CRAFTING
Wood Logic Puzzles

18 Three-Dimensional Games for the Hands & Mind

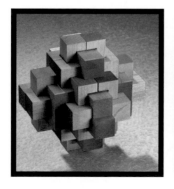

**Creative Publishing
international**

CHANHASSEN, MINNESOTA
www.creativepub.com

CONTENTS

Creative Publishing international

© Copyright 2006
Creative Publishing international, Inc.
18705 Lake Drive East
Chanhassen, Minnesota 55317
1-800-328-3895
www.creativepub.com
All rights reserved

Printed in China
10 9 8 7 6 5 4 3 2 1

President/CEO: Ken Fund
Vice President/Retail Sales & Marketing: Kevin Haas

Executive Editor: Bryan Trandem
Assistant Managing Editor: Tracy Stanley
Authors: Tom Lensch, Charles Self
Editors: Thomas Lemmer, Mark Johanson
Copy Editor: Karen Ruth
Art Director: Jon Simpson
Illustrator: Jon Simpson
Page Design: Bill Nelson
Photo Researcher: Julie Caruso
Photographer: Steve Galvin
Scene Shop Carpenter: Randy Austin
Production Manager: Linda Halls

WOOD LOGIC PUZZLES
ISBN 10: 1-58923-247-X
ISBN 13: 978-1-58923-247-1

Library of Congress
Cataloging-in-Publication Data

Self, Charles R.
    Crafting wood logic puzzles : 18 three-dimensional games for the hands &
mind / by Charlie Self with Tom Lensch.
        p. cm.
    Summary: "Provides plans and instructions for crafting 18 of the most pop-
ular manual puzzles. Projects range from traditional "put together/take apart"
games like pentominoes and soma cubes to more sophisticated "unlocking"
head-scratchers, such as the Burr puzzles. Readers will also learn special-
ized cutting, drilling, sanding, gluing, and finishing techniques that make
crafting wooden puzzles possible"--Provided by publisher.
    ISBN 1-58923-247-X (soft cover)
1. Wooden toy making. I. Lensch, Tom. II. Title.
    TT174.5.W6S44 2006
    745.592--dc22
                        2005030249

INTRODUCTION

Wood logic puzzles have been around for centuries. In times past, a broad selection of wood puzzles could be found on store shelves. But today, plastics have overtaken wood, and quality wood puzzles are available only in specialty shops.

Plastic will never approach the beauty of wood. The variety of wood species allows for many intriguing combinations. The warmth of most woods, along with the varied grain patterns and figures, provides each puzzle with a unique look. Nothing else looks exactly like puzzle no. 1 to come from your shop, and even if you use the same plans and jigs, nothing else looks like puzzle no. 500.

Great wood logic puzzles are those that draw people in by offering a feature that seems to make the solution especially difficult...or especially easy. Gauging frustration levels is important to successful puzzle design. Quick puzzle solvers will appreciate puzzles with more than one possible solution and puzzles where each piece is identical. The easily frustrated will be satisfied with simpler puzzles with a basic solution. Knowing your audience will increase your popularity as a puzzle maker.

If you wish to dramatically change the appearance of a puzzle, simply alternate wood types. Use a dark wood for half and a light wood for the other half. Or choose woods with contrasting color variations, from red or dark brown to near white or straw colored. You can also find woods with minimal figure or grain and position them next to highly figured woods. None of the puzzles here uses enough wood to make much difference in cost for your project. But if you get into rare and expensive woods like ebony, your expenses will definitely increase. Often, the jigs consume more wood than the puzzles.

Basic power woodworking skills, some standard tools, and strong attention to detail are the attributes that will allow you to pursue puzzle making as a new hobby or as a part of your existing woodworking craftwork. There's usually no need to invest in new or different tools, if you're already a woodworker. You may need to change the way you work to allow handling very small, very precise parts, but otherwise, little difference in skills is needed.

For any woodworker who enjoys modestly challenging projects and wants to develop skills in making precise setups and cuts, there aren't any better projects than wood logic puzzles. They are satisfying to make, satisfying to solve, and satisfying to give as gifts.

Because all of these puzzles include small parts, children who play with them should be at least three years old.

Basic Techniques

There are few mysteries to making wood logic puzzles, but there are tools and techniques that ease the work and reduce wasted time and stress during production. Precision and accuracy are key in crafting fun and attractive puzzles. Basic woodworking skills assisted by power tools, specialty jigs and a methodical approach will produce attractive wood puzzles. This chapter takes a quick look at the basic tools and techniques needed to make the eighteen puzzles included in this book.

Workshop Safety

Your arsenal of safety gear should include both hearing and eye protection. Buy comfortable styles so you'll wear them willingly whenever you're using machinery.

Wood dust is irritating to breathe and probably harmful to your health over the long haul. Wear a disposable respirator (A) or one with replaceable filters (B) to protect your lungs. When working with solvents and finishes, wear a canister solvent respirator (C).

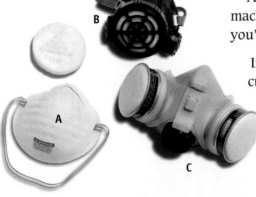

Shop accidents happen in an instant, especially with power tools. The danger is even greater when you're working with small pieces, such as those required for many of the projects in this book. The results can be irreversible and life-threatening. Your first line of defense against mishaps is simple: Think before doing. Respect the capabilities and dangers of your tools and know how to use them safely. Keep your tools in good repair and your bits and blades clean and sharp. Remove blade guards and other safety devices only when absolutely necessary. And keep the workspace clean and the floor clear of debris.

Personal safety gear will help you avoid accidents and work comfortably. Virtually every task that requires a tool creates some degree of danger for your eyes, and power tools can be damaging to your ears. Safety gear manufacturers offer a variety of different eye and ear protection devices to suit personal preference. When it comes to eye safety, purchase antifog safety glass or goggles that fit your face properly and protect your eyes from both the front and sides. Keep them clean and protect them from scratches when not in use. Hearing protection options range from earmuffs that cover your ears entirely to foam earplugs that fit inside your ear canal. Whichever style you choose, be sure it has a noise reduction rating (NRR) of at least 25 decibels, which is a safe standard for general power tool use.

Research suggests that wood dust can be a carcinogen, as well as an irritant. When using dust-producing machinery, especially saws and sanders, wear a respirator. Respirators approved for wood dusts are different from inexpensive, hospital-style nuisance masks, although they may look similar. Usually, dust respirators will have two head straps rather than one, and the packaging will clearly identify the product as a respirator. Dust masks actually offer little protection from fine wood dust. If you are working with solvent- or oil-based strippers, cleaners, or finishes, a dust respirator will not filter out the mists and fumes produced by these materials. Wear a respirator outfitted with replaceable canister filters rated for vapors and change the filters as soon as you can smell solvents through the mask.

As for other apparel, roll up long shirtsleeves to keep them clear of machinery and messes, and wear comfortable shoes with rubber soles if you'll be standing for long periods of time.

If you work alone in the shop, plan your woodworking sessions to occur when someone else is home and can check on you from time to time or lend a hand if necessary. To avoid accidents and mistakes, stop working if you are feeling tired, frustrated, or rushed. It should go without saying that it's never safe to operate woodworking machinery when you're under the influence of alcohol or other drugs that impair your judgment.

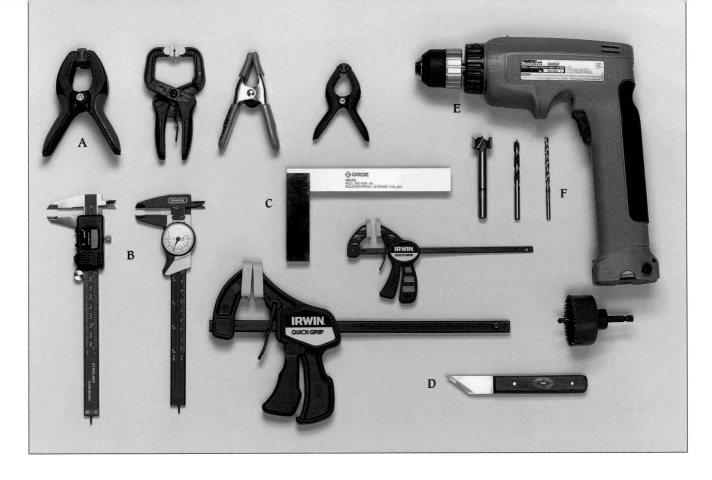

Tools for Crafting Wood Puzzles

The average woodworking shop may have all the basic tools required for making wood puzzles. For those who don't have everything, the following pages detail a variety of tools you'll use.

A. Clamps. Small, one-hand speed clamps and spring clamps hold small puzzle parts securely when drilling or gluing.

B. Dial or digital calipers. Precise measurement of specific puzzle pieces is a major ingredient in the success of many puzzles. An inexpensive dial caliper is accurate enough, although digital calipers are more accurate but not much more expensive.

C. Engineer's square. An 8" engineer's square is the most accurate square available at a reasonable cost, and a 4" size is also helpful. Engineer's squares are more accurate, and retain their accuracy better, than combination squares.

Cabinetmaker's rule. An 18" or 24" stainless steel cabinetmaker's rule makes more precise measurements than a tape measure or a wooden rule.

D. Marking knife. Use a marking knife instead of a pencil when possible. The finer line allows greater accuracy.

E. Cordless drills. While a drill press will handle all your accurate drilling needs, a cordless drill will come in most handy when building jigs for cutting and gluing.

F. Drill bits. There are a variety of drill bits that are important in crafting wood puzzles. Forstner bits bore exceptionally clean holes. They can drill at almost any angle, drill holes close to other holes, and create flat-bottomed holes. Brad-point bits, sometimes called "dowel bits," are less expensive and drill clean holes faster than Forstner bits. Twist bits, primarily for metalworking, offer a greater variation in bit sizes than brad-point and Forstner bits, and are useful for many basic woodworking chores. A set of each type of these bits will come in handy for crafting wood puzzles.

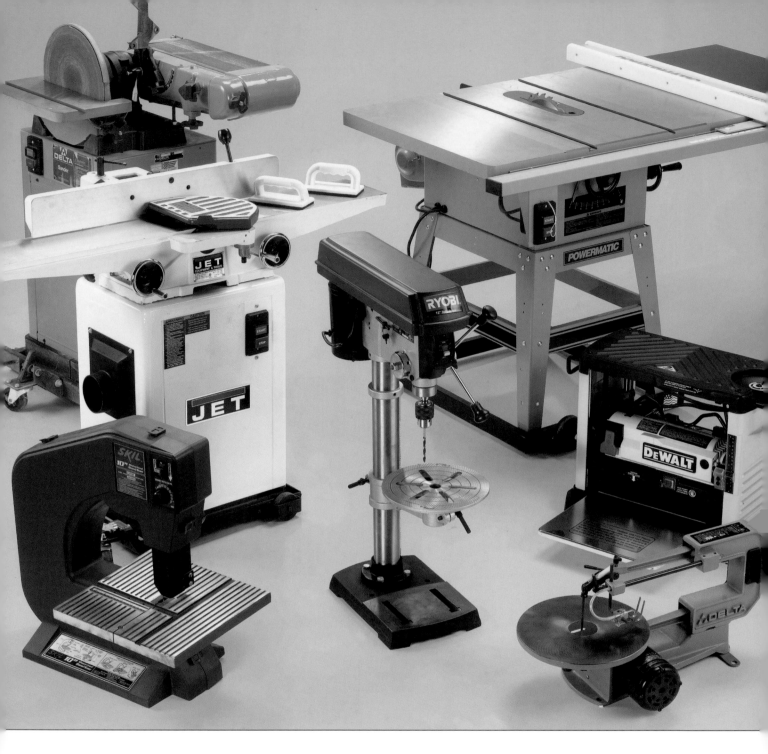

Table saw. Accurate cuts make good puzzles. A table saw is the easiest and most precise tool for the straight cuts needed in wood puzzles. Make sure your table saw has two miter slots, and that adjustment of the saw blade to those slots can be readily accomplished.

Use a 10" blade with a top-notch 40- or 50-tooth general-cut blade. Carbide tips on the teeth should be in an alternate top bevel (ATB) pattern for smoothest cutting and reducing tearout. There may be a triple chip grind every third or fourth tooth, and a raker to clean the kerf. Look for a hook angle on the teeth of about 12° to 15°.

Jointer. When using rough stock lumber (most hardwoods are sold rough), a jointer is the tool used to flatten one face of a narrow board, called "face jointing." This reference edge allows jointing the edge of the board at 90° to the face, or lets the planer produce a second face parallel to the face-jointed surface. The jointer does not produce parallel faces, so a planer is still needed. A good 6"-wide jointer is an essential puzzle making tool.

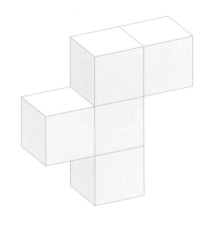

Planer. The planer, or thicknesser, planes boards to a set thickness. It is a one-trick pony, but that one trick can make the difference between success and failure in puzzle making. A good planer is needed for these puzzles even if you're working with surfaced wood. Small planers do custom thicknessing of any type of wood, making plans that call for $3/8$"- or $5/16$"- or $1/4$"-thick woods much more practical. The planer can also be used to make square sections absolutely square with a second pass on an adjoining side.

Drill press. For the puzzles included in this book, a 10" benchtop drill press is more than sufficient. Because most of the drilling required for wood puzzles is done with Forstner bits, which require a fairly low speed, the bottom end speed must be 500 RPM or lower. Horsepower (HP) needs are low; a press with $1/4$ HP does all the work. Of greater importance, however, is the accuracy of a particular combination of chuck and drill press.

While chucks can be replaced, starting with a good-quality chuck is wise. Runout (the inaccuracy of a drill bit running in a less than true circular pattern) is affected by both the spindle arbor and the chuck. Often, excessive runout is caused by nothing more than a poor fit between the two, or dirt caught on the spindle arbor. If you're seeing sloppy holes when using top-quality drill bits, pop out the chuck and clean it and the arbor. This can help reduce runout to acceptable levels.

Bandsaw. While we use a table saw for most of our cutting needs, a small or light-duty bandsaw of decent quality, with a $1/4$"- or $3/8$"-wide blade with 12 or 14 teeth per inch (TPI), can be a tremendous help in cutting small puzzle parts. Bandsaw blades cut with a thinner kerf and less tearout than table saw blades, providing cleaner finished cuts with less waste.

Scroll saw. For the couple of puzzles in this book that require you to cut curves, a scroll saw is an immense help. Because the curved shapes of these puzzles do not require the precision needed in other puzzles (where square or rectangular shapes must fit together firmly), the size of the scroll saw is of relative unimportance—even the smallest scroll saws have a 16" stock depth and at least a 1" cutting thickness capacity, more than is needed for any of the puzzles provided here. Quality scroll saws produce very little vibration, and may have additional features such as a light that shines on the cut line and a blower that clears sawdust. A handheld jig-saw can also be used to cut curves.

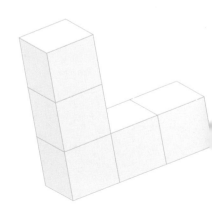

Belt/Disc Sanders. A small belt/disc sander is invaluable in shaping and cleaning up parts of most puzzles. Several companies offer models with a 4" × 36" belt and a 6" disc.

Truing the Table Saw Blade to 90°

You will make most of your cuts for wood puzzles with a table saw. To ensure accuracy in those cuts, you need to make sure the saw blade is perpendicular to the saw table. You will also want to make certain that the blade and the rip fence are parallel to the miter slots.

Before making any cuts with your table saw, check the vertical square of the saw blade, using an engineer's square that's at least 4" long. Crank the saw blade all the way up and set it at a 90° cutting angle. The square should fit flush against the blade, with the base flat on the table. Make sure you're not pressing the square's blade against a tooth. If the blade is not true, make any necessary adjustments (see your owner's manual) and reset the angle indicator to zero when alignment is correct.

For greater accuracy and safer cutting, the saw blade must be parallel to the miter slots, as well as to the rip fence. When the blade skews out of parallel, the condition is called blade heel. A heeling blade produces scorched edges and causes workpieces to wander away from the fence when you rip them. It makes cross-cutting and mitering difficult, as well. It's also a dangerous invitation for kickback.

Use an engineer's square to check the saw blade for square. Make adjustments as necessary.

You can adjust a rip fence so it's parallel to the saw blade, but that won't guarantee that either the rip fence or blade are parallel to the miter slots. A better method is to align the blade and miter slots first, then adjust the rip fence to the miter slots. This way, the blade and rip fence end up parallel to one another. The process for aligning the blade and miter slots involves shifting the entire saw table (on cabinet saws) or the arbor assembly (on contractor's saws) one way or the other until the blade and miter slots align. Doing this may seem cumbersome and nitpicky, but even 1/32" of adjustment will produce smoother, easier cutting with fewer burn marks. Plus, it's a tune-up procedure you'll probably need to make only once or rarely over the life of the machine.

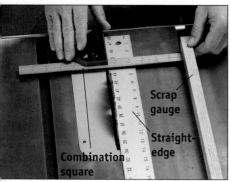

Scrap gauge

Straight-edge

Combination square

Use a combination square set against a straightedge and piece of scrap wood as a gauge for checking the blade's alignment to the miter slots. The scrap wood should fit snugly in the miter slot, and the straightedge should rest against the blade body. If the measurements in front and at back of the saw table are not the same, the blade is heeling relative to the miter slots.

Here's how to check if your blade is heeling relative to the miter slots: Find or mill a strip of hardwood that's about 1½" wide, 3 feet long, and fits snugly into the miter slots. The wood strip serves as a raised indicator for the miter slot positions. Set the strip into the miter slot you use most often—typically this is the one to the left of the blade if the blade tilts right, or the right slot for left-tilting saws. Crank the blade up to full height, and check that it's set to 90° using a combination or try square. Lay a reliably flat 3-foot straightedge against the blade body—not the carbide teeth. Lay a combination square on the saw table so its head is against the same reference edge on the straightedge as the blade. Position the square near the front of the saw table. Now extend the rule on the square until it touches the wooden strip, and lock the rule at this measurement. Be careful not to jar the straightedge away from the blade as you do this. Then shift the square to the back of the saw table and position it against the straightedge again. With the square's rule still locked in place, does the end of the rule touch the wood strip? If the rule comes up short or pushes the square's head off the straightedge, you'll know the blade is heeling further from or closer to the miter slots. If you are lucky enough to have the rule just touch the wooden strip, skip the following procedure for eliminating blade heel.

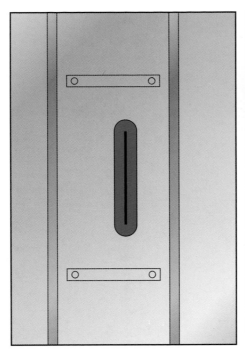

To eliminate blade heel, loosen three of the four bolts that mount the arbor and trunnion assembly to the underside of a contractor's saw (left), or three of four bolts securing the saw table to the base on a cabinet saw (right). Shift the sub-assembly or tabletop, retest for blade heel, then retighten the bolts.

If you're adjusting a cabinet saw, locate the four bolts that secure the saw table to the base, and loosen three of the four. On contractor's saws, find the four bolts that mount the arbor and trunnion assembly to the underside of the saw table. Loosen three of these bolts. Pivot the table of your cabinet saw or tap the trunnion on your contractor's saw to shift these components, and recheck the alignment of the blade and miter slots. Use the combination square and wooden strip method to check your progress. Remember that the amount you need to shift the table or arbor assembly is probably miniscule, so work gently. A tap or two with a rubber mallet or hammer and wood block may be all it takes. When you're making the adjustment on a contractor's saw, it's tough to tap the trunnion assembly if you're working inside the saw base from below. Use a wood block and rap down through the throat plate opening instead, or work from behind the saw. When the blade and miter slots line up, retighten the mounting bolts.

Now that your blade is parallel to the miter slots, you can eliminate all sources of heeling by adjusting the rip fence so it's also parallel to the miter slots. Fence designs vary in terms of where the adjustment bolts or screws are located. Older fences have two bolts on top of the fence body, while newer fences may have adjustment screws on the outside of the fence or on the big clamp that holds the fence on the front rail. Check your owner's manual to locate the adjusters on your fence.

To make the adjustment, slip a pair of 1½"- to 2"-wide wood blocks into one of the miter slots. The blocks should fit without extra play. Place one near the front of the saw and the other at the back. Slide the rip fence until it touches one or both blocks. You'll know the fence is parallel to the

With the mounting bolts loosened, tap the trunnion assembly on a contractor's saw through the throat plate opening using a block of wood and a hammer. This will shift the blade arbor in relation to the miter slots.

Check the alignment of the rip fence by placing it against blocks of wood in the miter slot. The rip fence should touch both blocks evenly. If it doesn't, adjust the fence until it does.

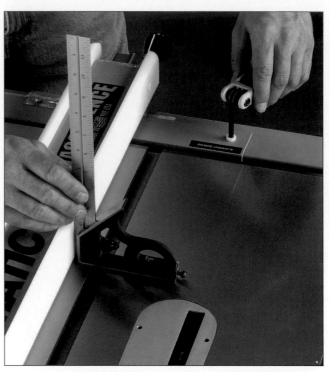

Use a square to see whether the rip fence face meets the saw table at 90°. Using the fence setscrews, tune the fence until it meets the table squarely. For a fence without setscrews, insert shims behind the faces.

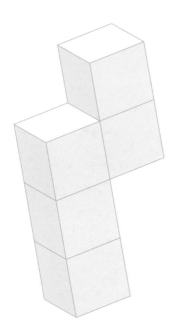

miter slot if it touches both blocks simultaneously. If it touches just one block, loosen the adjustment bolts or back out the adjustment screws and shift the fence body until it also touches the second block. Tighten the adjustment bolts or snug up the screws to hold the fence in this new position. Check the action of the fence by clamping it to the front rail. The fence body should remain parallel to the miter slot. If it doesn't, readjust the bolts or screws and try clamping it down again. Some low-quality fences simply won't stay aligned. If your saw has one of these, consider replacing it with a better aftermarket fence. Otherwise, the fence will never yield accurate cuts.

In addition to being parallel to the miter slots, the rip fence must also be square to the saw table. Check yours by standing a square on the saw table and against the fence face. If the fence tips into or away from the square, you may be able to adjust this condition by turning setscrews on the fence clamp. Otherwise, you can square up a fence by attaching a piece of plywood or hardwood to the fence to act as an auxiliary fence, then inserting a few slips of paper or aluminum soda cans behind the auxiliary fence to bring the fence faces into square.

Making a Crosscut Jig

For accuracy and safety when making cuts to small pieces of wood, cutting jigs are a necessity. The two most common jigs you'll use for the puzzle in this book are a basic crosscut jig and a dado-notching jig (see pages 18 to 19).

A basic crosscut jig (often called a crosscut sled) is simply a piece of plywood or MDF with tall rails along both front and back edges and mounted to glides that fit in the miter slots. A saw kerf or slot divides the middle of the base to provide a clear track for the blade. Jigs can be constructed to be as simple or as complex as needed.

To use the jig, place workpieces inside the jig and against the back rail, then slide the jig across the table to make the cut. Crosscut jigs provide several advantages over miter gauges. They provide a larger support area and the long back rail helps minimize splintering, or tearout. Once the back rail is set perpendicular to the saw blade, the jig never needs readjustment to make perfect square cuts.

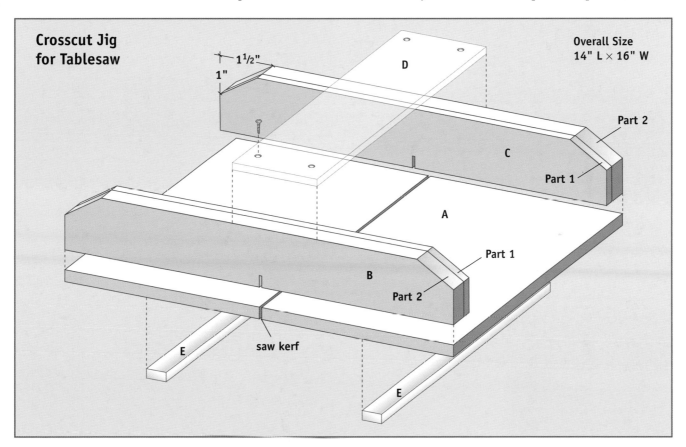

Crosscut Jig for Tablesaw

Overall Size 14" L × 16" W

1½"
1"
D
C
Part 2
Part 1
A
Part 1
B
Part 2
E
saw kerf
E

CUTTING LIST:

Key	Part	Size	Material	Number
A	Base	½" × 14" × 16"	MDF	1
B	Front rail (part 1)	½" × 3" × 16"	Baltic birch	1
	Front rail (part 2)	¾" × 3" × 16"	Baltic birch	1
C	Back rail (part 1)	½" × 3" × 16"	Baltic birch	1
	Back rail (part 2)	¾" × 3" × 16"	Baltic birch	1
D	Shield section	¼" × 3½" × 14"	Plexiglass	1
E	Miter slot slides	⅜" × ¾" × 14"	HDPE* plastic	2

*HDPE (high-density polyethylene) plastic is sold at some craft stores. If you are unable to find any, use an old plastic cutting board that's around ⅜" thick.

TOOLS & MATERIALS:

Tools: Cabinetmaker's rule, engineer's square, pencil, table saw, clamps, cordless drill, countersink

Materials: #6 × 1½" flathead screws (8), #6 × ¾" brass flathead screws (10), ½" panhead screws (4), plexiglass, HDPE plastic strips, wood glue, double-sided tape

How to Make a Crosscut Jig

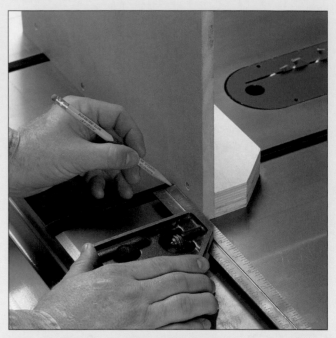

1 Cut the 14" × 16" jig base from ½" MDF. The front and back rails are made from laminated layers of ½" and ¾" plywood (you can use two layers of ¾"-thick material if you prefer). Cut the four rail pieces to 3" × 16" and face-glue them into two matching strips. Trim off the top corners of each rail (see drawing, page 15), then drill countersunk pilot holes and fasten the rails to the jig base with glue and using 1½" flathead screws.

2 Set the jig back rail down over the miter slots of the table saw, and center the jig base on the saw blade. Mark the location of one miter slot onto the underside of the jig base.

3 Cut two ¾" × 14" miter slot slides from ⅜" HDPE (high-density polyethylene) plastic. Drill countersunk pilot holes and fasten a slide to the base at the mark, using #6 × ¾" brass flathead screws (brass won't scratch your saw table). Do not attach the second slide yet.

4 Set a couple of pennies in the second miter slot, place a few small pieces of double-sided tape on the top edge of the second slide, and position the second slide in the slot on top of the pennies, tape up.

5 Set the jig in place, with the first slide in the first miter slot and the back of the jig flush with the back edge of the saw table. Push the jig down over the second slide, so the double-sided tape adheres to the bottom of the jig. Remove the jig, drill countersunk pilot holes and fasten the second slide to the jig base with the flathead screws.

6 Position the jig in the miter slots and feed it into the saw blade to create a blade clearance slot through the rails and base.

Stop

7 Cut a 3¹/₂" × 14" safety guard from ¹/₈"-thick plexiglass. Center the guard over the blade slot, then drill pilot holes and fasten it to the rails using ¹/₂" panhead screws. Do not overdrive the screws.

Tip: To make a length stop for making repetitive cuts, cut a 1¹/₂" × 1¹/₂" × 12" piece of hardwood square at the ends, then clamp it securely to the back rail of the jig.

Variation: Making a Dado-notching Jig

In addition to square straight cuts, some projects, such as the Chuck Puzzle (page 76), require notched or half-lap puzzle parts. The simple cross-cut jig shown on the previous pages (15 to 17) can easily be modified to create a sled for cutting notches, half-laps, or dadoes with a dado blade set installed in your table saw.

Anyone who has used an adjustable dado blade set can attest to the difficulty of getting a smooth-bottom cut. The upward force of the cutters can cause the workpiece to bounce slightly, even when it is clamped. For cleaner notches and half-laps, make at least two passes at the final depth and try using a toggle clamp as a hold-down (see below).

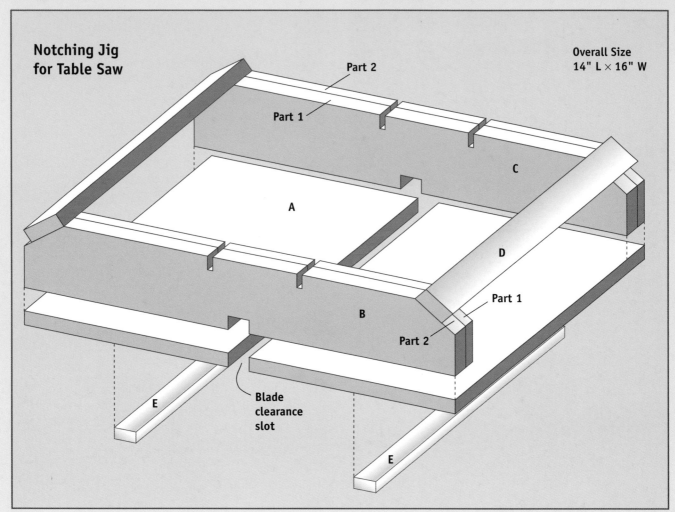

Notching Jig for Table Saw

Part 2
Part 1
C
A
D
B
Part 1
Part 2
E
Blade clearance slot
E

Overall Size
14" L × 16" W

CUTTING LIST:

Key	Part	Size	Material	Number
A	Base	1/2" × 14" × 16"	MDF	1
B	Front rail (part 1)	1/2" × 3" × 16"	Baltic birch	1
	Front rail (part 2)	3/4" × 3" × 16"	Baltic birch	1
C	Back rail (part 1)	1/2" × 3" × 16"	Baltic birch	1
	Back rail (part 2)	3/4" × 3" × 16"	Baltic birch	1
D	Side rail	1/2" × 1 1/4" × 14"	Baltic birch	2
E	Miter slot slides	3/8" × 3/4" × 14"	HDPE* plastic	2

*HDPE (high-density polyethylene) plastic is sold at some craft stores. If you are unable to find any, use an old plastic cutting board that's around 3/8" thick.

TOOLS & MATERIALS:

Tools: Cabinetmaker's rule, engineer's square, pencil, table saw, clamps, cordless drill, countersink

Materials: #6 × 1 1/2" flathead screws (8), #6 × 3/4" brass flathead screws (10), HDPE plastic strips, wood glue, double-sided tape

How to Make a Notching Jig

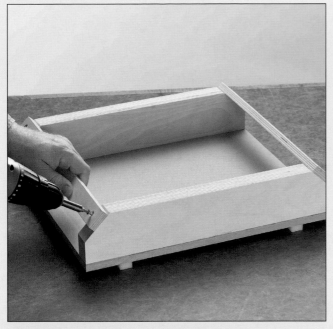

1 Follow steps 1 to 5 of "How to Make a Crosscut Jig" (pages 16 to 17) to build the body of the jig. Cut two $1/2" \times 1^1/4" \times 14"$ side rails from Baltic birch to serve as handles for the notching jig, then drill pilot holes and fasten the side rails at the angled corners of the front and back rails.

2 Mount a dado blade set in your table saw. Before cutting the blade clearance slot in the jig, test the width of the cut on a piece of scrap. Make adjustments to the dado blade cutting width as necessary, then raise the saw blade and cut the clearance slot, making multiple passes and raising the blade set with each pass until you reach full depth.

3 To ensure safe cutting, help reduce tearout, and ease cutting multiple pieces, cut a clamp body access slot in the back rail, 1" from the blade clearance slot on each side, to accommodate a pair of quick-grip clamps.

Toggle option: Attach a vertical toggle clamp to the jig base to secure workpieces or length stops. This method will accommodate a variety of wood thicknesses and provide downward pressure that prevents the workpiece from bouncing (a common occurrence with dado sets).

Basic woods include: (A) birch, (B) ash, (C) cherry, (D) white oak, (E) maple, (F) mahogany, (G) red oak, and (H) walnut.

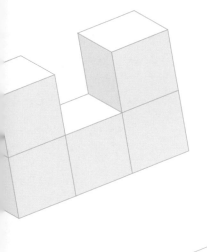

Selecting Wood for Puzzles

Choosing woods is an important part of any woodworking project, including puzzle making. Start by sorting through your shop scrap barrel or pile to see what has been tossed aside from larger projects. Look for hardwoods, especially hardwoods that don't dent easily. For wood that will be planed, 24" or longer lengths are best. Many planers, especially older models, snipe the ends of the wood, ruining 2½" to 3½" of each piece, so try to take that into account.

Select woods for appearance, durability, workability, and stainability. Whether your wood stock is milled to standard dimensions or rough sawn, you should prepare the workpieces yourself to ensure accurate puzzle pieces. For most of the puzzles, look for boards with an actual thickness between ¾" and 5⁄4".

You'll find many color and pattern variations in wood that can add to the attractiveness and the uniqueness of your puzzles. The most commonly available woods are walnut, cherry, oak, ash, and maple, although the list varies somewhat according to where you live. Walnut is a dark wood, often ranging toward dark purple when first cut. It will gradually lighten as it ages. Cherry often has a salmon color, depending on whether it is heartwood (darker) or sapwood (lighter). Over time, cherry darkens. White oak is light tan and red oak has a reddish hue. Both oaks have a distinct grain pattern, especially if quarter-sawn. Ash has grain and figure similar to the oaks, but is lighter. Hard maple has many attractive grain and figure patterns. Hickory, though excellent for tool handles, is best avoided when crafting because it is splintery and hard to work.

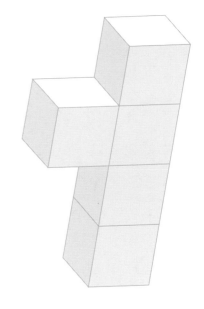

Other rarer domestic hardwoods are available from specialty lumber suppliers. They include mesquite, which is hard to dent and very stable. Holly can be hard to find, but is almost white, which is a unique look. California laurel (also called Pacific myrtle) is a very hard and heavy tan wood that is close grained and often has bird's-eye figures and swirls. Tupelo, or black gum, is a light brown wood with a fine texture and interlocked grain that keeps it from splitting.

Exotic woods for puzzles abound. Mahogany is a premium wood for puzzles because it has excellent dimensional stability so the puzzle pieces fit together properly in all conditions. In the super-expensive arena is ebony, a rare black wood. It is hard to glue, which needs to be kept in mind (epoxy works). Bubinga is another exotic that is good for puzzles. Cocobolo is a relative of rosewood, from Central America. It is oily, thus hard to glue, and is hard on tools due to silica inclusions. Additionally, it is expensive, and many people are allergic to its dust. Padauk, a hard, heavy wood with interlocking grain, ages to a dark maroon color. It is an excellent puzzle wood. Purple heart is another useful exotic puzzle wood. It mellows to a rich, red-brown final color after a bright purple look on first cutting. Rosewoods are becoming rare, and they are hard to work and glue, but make lovely puzzles. Ziricote (also called zebra wood) is a dark wood, heavy, hard, with black streaks on a tan background. It is oily and hard to glue, as well hard to find and expensive. Nevertheless, it is attractive and useful. Satinwood works nicely, too, as do bloodwood, bocote, and canary wood.

Exotic woods include:
(A) Lacewood, (B) padauk, (C) purple heart, (D) teak, (E) cocobolo, (F) wenge, (G) Brazilian cherry, (H) zebra wood, (I) bocote, (J) bloodwood, (k) canary wood, (L) dark rosewood, and (M) bloodwood.

Preparing Wood Stock

Preparing wood stock for use in a puzzle starts with surfacing lumber to the widths and thicknesses specified in the project plans and cutting list. If the tolerances in the plan are tight, such as with the Melting Block Puzzle (pages 110 to 113), make the puzzle from a stable wood, such as white oak or mahogany.

As you select your wood stock, make sure to work with boards that are at least 24" long if they will be jointed or planed for puzzle pieces requiring specific and accurate dimensions. You can cut stock to rough length as needed, however it will be cut down to usable lengths and shapes later (see page 24). If stock is to be planed, make sure to allow an extra 3" to 4" for snipe, the shallow dished-out area caused by the planer taking a slightly deeper bite from the ends of boards when the feed rollers grab or release the lumber as it passes through the planer.

The first step in preparing wood for puzzles is to face-joint the stock to achieve a uniform reference

Snipe is the result of a planer taking a slightly deeper bite from the ends of boards as they pass through the feed rollers. Make sure to account for snipe when planning puzzles.

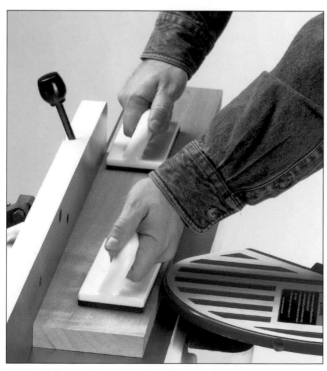

To face joint stock, use push sticks or push pads to guide the board over the jointer knives while keeping your hands clear.

Use a power planer to reduce your workpieces to rough thickness initially and then to final thickness.

surface. Set the jointer to a cutting depth of 1/32" and adjust the fence so it's square with the jointer bed. Hold the board face flat against the jointer bed and use push sticks or push pads to guide the stock over the jointer knives and to keep your hands clear. For particularly rough or uneven lumber, you may need to take several passes to flatten the face.

The next step is to plane the stock to rough thickness—the finished dimension plus 1/32". Use a dial or digital caliper to determine the actual thickness of the stock, then set the planer's cutterhead so it will trim the board about 1/16" thinner. However, for many hardwoods you may need to take an even shallower pass to keep the planer's motor from bogging down.

After face-jointing the workpiece, joint one edge to ensure that it is flat and square.

Feed the board into the planer with the reference face against the smooth planer bed to plane the other face. Check the board thickness with the dial caliper, then drop the cutterhead another 1/16" or less as needed and repeat until you have created a board with two smooth, parallel faces and a thickness that is 1/32" more than the final dimensions specified in the project plans.

Finally, joint one edge of the board to create a square reference edge. You can now rip the stock to the width dimension specified in the project plans, remembering to allow an extra 1/32" to allow for final planing and sanding.

Ripping Boards Into Usable Shapes

After the wood stock has been jointed and planed to within 1/32" of the finished puzzle dimensions (see pages 22 to 23), the boards can be ripped into the sticks from which the finished squares and rectangles that make up the bulk of the puzzle pieces will be cut.

First rip the boards into sticks that are 1/32" wider than the finished width of the puzzle piece called for in the project plans. Use featherboards to help keep workpieces pressed firmly against the saw table and rip fence as they enter the blade. Clamp one featherboard to the saw table on the infeed side of the blade, then clamp a second featherboard to the rip fence so it lines up with the one mounted to the saw table. Position both featherboards just far enough from the blade so they won't interfere with the blade guard; Adjust both so they hold the workpiece firmly but not so tightly that they restrict your ability to push the board forward.

Once cut to rough width, the sticks should be square, though 1/32" larger than the dimensions of the finished puzzle pieces. Check for accuracy using dial calipers. If final planing or jointing are required, make sure the sticks are at least 24" long. When cutting multiple puzzle parts from a single stick, be sure to allow 1/8" for each saw kerf and an extra inch or two for waste.

Wood for puzzles such as the Dagger Puzzle, Two Rings Puzzle, and Tower of Hanoi can be cut to the finished length and width, provided the stock has been planed to the exact thickness specified in the project plans. These puzzles do not require perfectly square or rectangular pieces for fine fitting, such as the Notched Packing Puzzle.

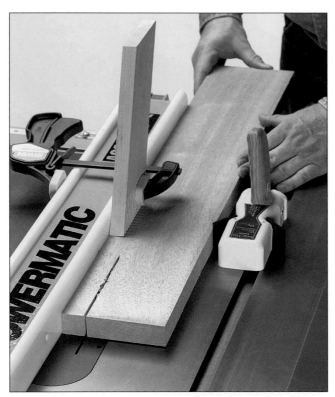

Featherboards clamped to the rip fence and saw table hold workpieces securely during rip cutting. Be sure to install them just in front of the blade—not behind it.

Use a dial calipers to check stick dimensions to ensure accurate measurements.

Forming Wood Squares and Rectangles

Accurate wood squares and rectangles are produced using the planer and table saw. For final sizing, set the table saw rip fence to the exact final size as specified in the project plans. Run a scrap piece of lumber through the saw and check the cut piece for accuracy with a dial caliper. Make adjustments as needed, but make sure to verify using the scrap piece. With saw set, run each stick through twice, once for the first side and a second pass on the adjacent side. This will produce sticks that are perfectly square and ready to be cut to length for puzzle parts.

Variation: If you don't want to use a table saw, you can get the same results by running sticks through the planer—once on each adjacent side.

When the finished sticks are ready to be cut into the square or rectangle puzzle parts, they can be taped together securely using easy-release (blue) masking tape to reduce the need for multiple cuts. The parts must be tightly taped for accuracy. It's possible to easily cut as many as six small sticks at one time if taping is tightly done.

To cut the squares and rectangles, simply set a length stop on the crosscut jig (see pages 15 to 17) to the finished length, cut a scrap piece and check for accuracy with a dial caliper, then make your cuts.

Use the table saw to rip sticks to the final puzzle dimensions by shaving ¹⁄₃₂″ off two adjacent sides.

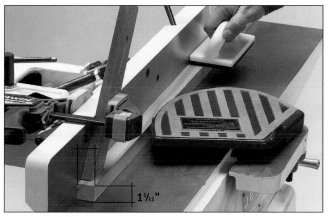

A jointer or power planer can also be used to bring sticks to final dimensions.

To gang-cut multiple sticks for puzzle parts, use easy-release masking tape to bind the workpieces tightly.

Use a crosscut jig to efficiently cut ganged puzzle parts to their finished lengths.

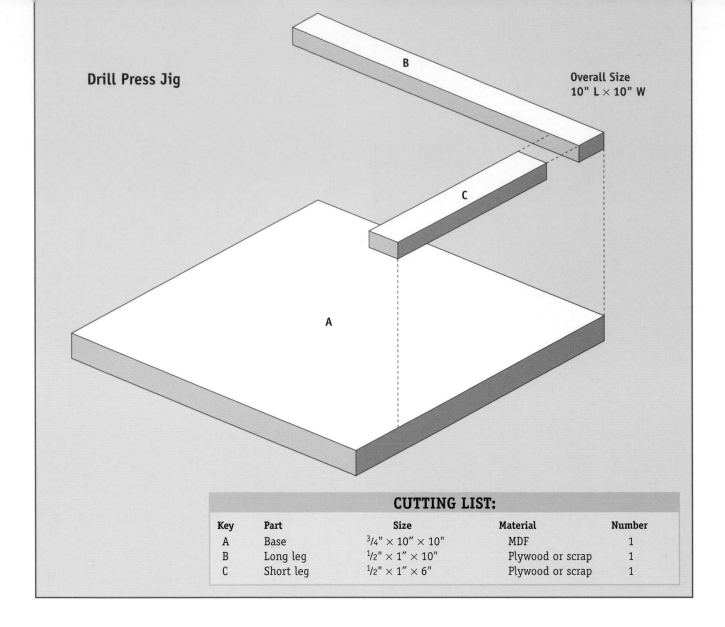

Drill Press Jig

B

Overall Size
10" L × 10" W

C

A

CUTTING LIST:				
Key	Part	Size	Material	Number
A	Base	$3/4" \times 10" \times 10"$	MDF	1
B	Long leg	$1/2" \times 1" \times 10"$	Plywood or scrap	1
C	Short leg	$1/2" \times 1" \times 6"$	Plywood or scrap	1

Drilling

Drilling operations in puzzle pieces usually involve holding small pieces of the project so they cannot spin or get tossed off the drill table. The simple jigs shown here hold square, rectangular, and spherical pieces securely in place for safe, accurate drilling.

How to Make a Drilling Jig for Square and Rectangular Parts

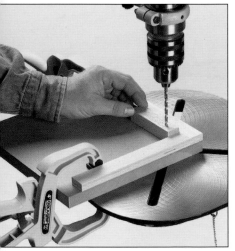

A simple square corner jig makes it easier to drill accurate holes in square and rectangular puzzle parts.

Cut the jig base from ¾" MDF and the legs from ½" plywood (such as baltic birch) or scrap material, to the dimensions specified in the cutting list above. All pieces must be perfectly square. To assemble the jig, simply glue the legs to the base, flush with the edges, to create the right angle. Use an engineer's square to ensure that the legs meet at a perfect right angle (90°). After the glue dries, the jig is ready for use and can be clamped in position to the drill press table. Place the workpiece squarely in a corner, then simply hold or clamp the piece in place as you drill. To protect the MDF base use a backer board beneath the workpiece.

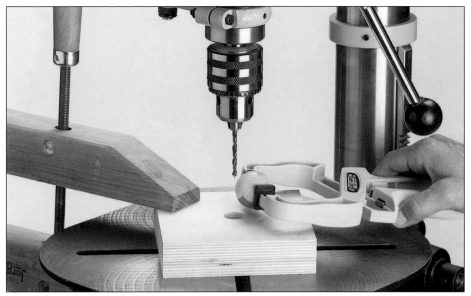

Drill a ½"- to ⅝"-deep hole with a ⅞" Forstner bit into a 1½"-thick scrap board to create a jig for holding wooden balls.

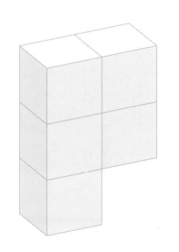

How to Make a Drilling Jig to Hold Wooden Balls

A few puzzles require that you drill holes through wooden balls, which can be a challenge. The easiest approach is to make a quick jig using a scrap of wood.

Clamp a 6" × 6" × 1½" scrap of wood to the drill table, and drill a ½"- to ⅝"-deep hole in the center, using a ⅞" Forstner bit. Wrap the bottom of a wooden ball with two layers of easy-release masking tape to reduce splintering when the bit exits the ball, and set the ball in the hole of the jig.

Clamp the ball so it can't spin, using a handscrew-style clamp or another clamp with a fairly wide mouth. If necessary, use a second clamp to hold the first clamp under the drill bit. Set the drill press depth so the balls can be added and removed from the jig easily. Then drill through the ball, using a brad-point bit.

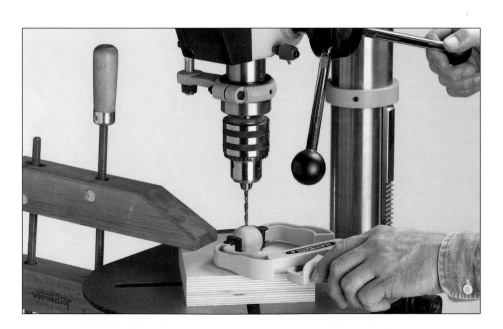

When drilling holes, hold the wooden ball in place with a clamp and use a brad-point bit.

Gluing and Clamping

You don't need a huge variety of glues for puzzle making. Standard yellow wood glue (polyvinyl acetate, or PVA), works fine for all the puzzles shown in this book. It is moderately moisture resistant (for places where it is damp indoors), easy to use, and inexpensive. It creates a strong bond and the glue line is barely visible.

Most yellow glues require 45 minutes to an hour of setup time. It does not hurt to extend that time an hour or so, especially in damp weather. Do not apply stress to any glued joints for at least 12 hours. Read the instructions on your glue bottle for further information. Creating neat, strong glue joints does take some practice.

To glue up puzzle parts, apply yellow glue sparingly to both sides of the joint, and make sure there is no slopover at all. For most joints, use a flat-edged piece of scrap wood or a Popsicle stick as a spreader. Wipe the edges with a rag before joining the pieces, then clamp together with light pressure, or simply set the parts aside in one of the gluing jigs (see pages 30 to 31). If any glue squeezes out of the joints, let it dry and remove with a razor blade or by sanding.

For oily exotic woods, use epoxy. Epoxy is expensive, and it requires care in use, but only small amounts are needed. Using a slow set (ten minutes) epoxy is best, along with light clamping to hold the parts in position. On oily exotic woods, even epoxy works better if the joint surfaces get a light wipe down with acetone or alcohol just before the adhesive is applied.

Spread glue carefully, onto both mating wood surfaces, using a glue spreader or glue brush.

Use small clamps like this mini quick-release clamp to press glue joints together while the glue sets up.

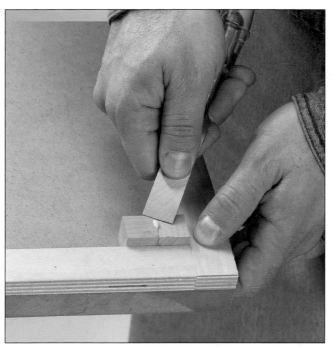

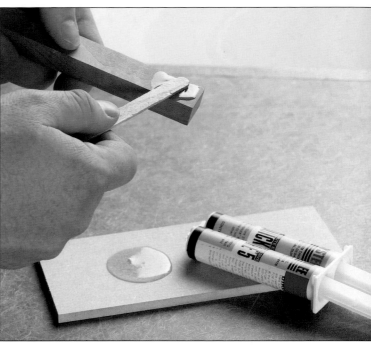

Scrape or shave glue squeezeout after it dries using a sharp chisel. Do not try to wipe off excess glue while it is wet—you'll only drive it more deeply into the wood pores.

Spread epoxy neatly and carefully—Epoxy drips are very hard to remove.

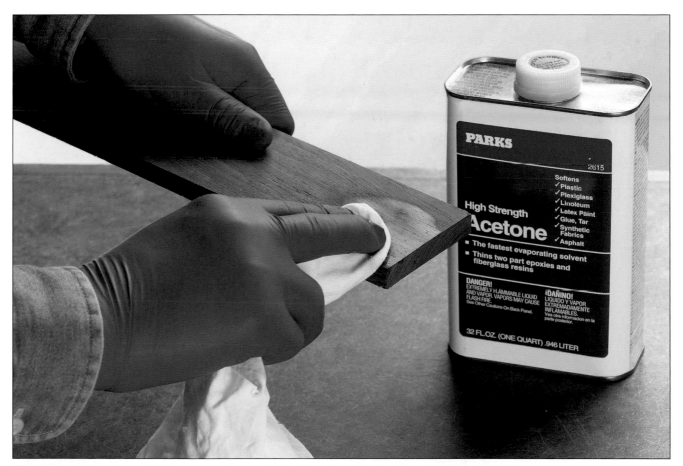

Wipe down oily exotic woods like rosewood or cocobolo with acetone to clean the surface of oils.

How to Make a Square Corner Gluing Jig

Cut a ¼" notch into each jig leg, one at ½" in from the end, and the other at 3" from the end. The notches make removing parts easier if they are accidentally glued to the jig legs.

To make a square corner gluing jig, cut two 2½" × 7½" legs from ¾" Baltic birch. Set the table saw blade height to ¾" and use the crosscut jig (pages 15 to 17) to cut notches in each piece. On the first leg, cut the notch at ½" from one end, and on the second leg, cut the notch at 3" from one end. These notches make it easier to separate the parts from the jig if glue has seeped through.

To construct the jig, simply glue the ½" notched end of the first leg to the side of the second leg with the 3" notch, clamp, and allow the glue to dry. Make sure the edges of the pieces are flush and that the inside corner creates a ½" × ½" corner along the legs before the notches.

To use the jig, clamp it to a piece of HDPE plastic or a piece of flat tempered glass to help prevent any glue that has seeped from the joints of the puzzle parts from adhering to the surface. Glue up your squares into the shape specified in the project plans and then set them in place against the jig. Use clamps with light pressure to hold pieces together.

TIP BOX:

Tip: To ensure excess glue will not bond with the jigs, rub the jig surfaces with paraffin wax and smooth out; the glue will not stick to waxed surfaces.

This corner gluing jig offers secure perpendicular surfaces to help you align small parts when gluing them together.

How to Make a Cube-corner Gluing Jig

To create a gluing jig for the more complex geometric shapes of puzzles like the Soma Cube (page 48) and Half-hour Puzzle (page 54), cut the base and two sides from ¾" Baltic birch plywood and fasten together, following the cutting list and illustration to the right. Make sure all the parts are perfectly square to ensure accuracy of the puzzle shapes. Also cut a 3¾" × 3¾" movable insert plate from ¾" hardwood, or the same thickness as the wood squares you are using. The plate eases removal of shapes that have accidentally been glued to the jig.

To use the cube-corner gluing jig, glue the wood squares into one of the cube shapes shown in the project plans. Place the jig plate on the base and into the corner, then set the shape into the corner of the jig. For complex shapes, use extra wood squares as needed to help the new shape hold its form. Apply light pressure with small clamps.

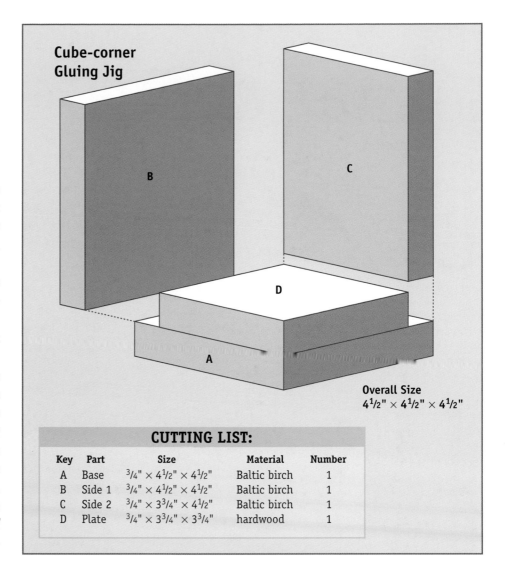

Cube-corner Gluing Jig

Overall Size
4½" × 4½" × 4½"

CUTTING LIST:

Key	Part	Size	Material	Number
A	Base	¾" × 4½" × 4½"	Baltic birch	1
B	Side 1	¾" × 4½" × 4½"	Baltic birch	1
C	Side 2	¾" × 3¾" × 4½"	Baltic birch	1
D	Plate	¾" × 3¾" × 3¾"	hardwood	1

Construct a cube-corner gluing jig to form the shapes of 3D cube puzzles.

Sanding

Generally, light sanding is all that is needed, as puzzle parts are cut very close to finished size. Most sanding is done by hand and does little more than remove the fuzz at a saw cut's edge. Specialty sanding accessories, such as flap sander heads, can be useful for sanding complex shapes with little degradation of the shape. But for sanding flat surfaces and edges, a small sanding block is the only tool you'll really need.

Well chosen sanding products take some of the chore out of sanding. In addition to conventional sandpaper, you can use sanding blocks, sponges, contour sanders, sanding cord, and sanding belts.

Sanding blocks are available at home centers and hardware stores, but you can simply use a 4" scrap of 2 × 4. For best results, joint the edges of a 10" or longer piece of 2 × 4 to a width of 3¼", face-joint to remove the rounded corners and create square edges, then cut the piece down to a manageable 4" block. Simply wrap sandpaper around the block tightly and hold it in place as you sand. For added stability, staple the paper to the block—but take care not to sand surfaces with the stapled side of the sanding block.

As with any sanding, always work with the wood grain. Use quality open-grit garnet sandpapers, ranging from 120-grit to 220-grit. For most puzzle parts, begin with a 180-grit paper and work up to only 220-grit to prevent losing too much size or shape. For rougher stock or puzzle parts that do not require tight fittings, you can start with 120-grit and work up through 150-grit, 180-grit, and finally 220-grit.

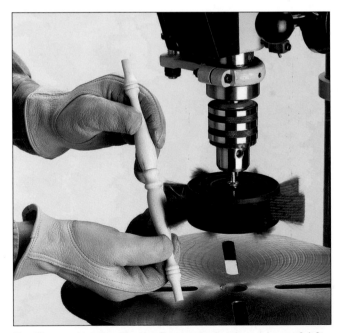

Sanding accessories like the flap sander heads can be useful for sanding the often complex and irregular shapes of wood puzzle parts.

A scrap piece of 2 × 4 can make an effective sanding block. You can also purchase sanding blocks at any home center.

Penetrating oil produces an attractive finish without altering the finished sizes of tight-fitting puzzle parts by raising grain, as some finishes do. Popular penetrating oils for puzzles include Danish oil, tung oil, boiled linseed oil, and teak oil.

Finishing

A well-accomplished finish is very important to the appearance and durability of a wood puzzle. But be aware that many popular finishes, such as lacquers and polyurethane varnish, have physical thickness that can interfere with the fit of the intricate pieces—sometimes enough to make a puzzle unworkable. Finishes that do not create a finish layer, such as penetrating oils, are best for puzzles. These include Danish oil, tung oil, boiled linseed oil, and teak oil.

Most penetrating oils are simply wiped onto the wood surface using a cloth or brush. The finish is allowed to penetrate into the wood pores and then the excess is wiped off so the finish can cure. A second coat can be applied if you are unhappy with the evenness or gloss of the first coat, but keep in mind that the more coats you apply, the more prone a part is to developing some surface buildup. Always follow the manufacturer's recommendations and check the fit of parts between each application of finishing product.

Most penetrating oil finishes can be brushed on or wiped on. Wear nitrile or latex gloves when applying oil-base finishes.

If several coats of oil are desired, wipe off the residue from the first coat after fifteen minutes and then apply the second coat.

Wood Puzzle Projects

The following chapter contains plans and instructions for crafting eighteen classic wood logic puzzles that will both challenge your woodworking skills and offer users many hours of healthy, frustrating fun. The projects are presented more or less in order of construction difficulty—the easiest projects first, the more difficult ones later—though none of the puzzles is beyond the ability or means of the patient woodworker. The key to creating attractive puzzles comes down to wood selection—species that contrast in color (holly and padauk) or woods that have extraordinary grain or figure (hard maple, oak, or mahogany) will result in visually appealing puzzles that will be enjoyed, admired, and tested by family and friends for years to come.

Two Rings Puzzle

One of the simplest of all wood logic puzzles to make (but not necessarily to solve) is the Two Rings Puzzle. With basic shop skills and very little material you can create a puzzle that is wonderfully frustrating. The object of Two Rings is to move one ring from one loop of string and onto the other loop so both rings hang from the same loop. The challenge is complicated by the fact that the hole in the center of the wood block is too small for the rings to pass through it. The solution for this puzzle can be found on page 116.

Because the Two Rings Puzzle does not require accurate measurements for tight-fitting pieces, the body of the puzzle can be fashioned from any type of wood in almost any shape. Even the brass rings can be swapped for different materials, sizes, or objects such as beads, so long as the objects cannot pass through the hole in the center of the body. See page 39 for variations of this puzzle.

TOOLS & MATERIALS

Materials: 1" × 3" hardwood board; sandpaper, various grit; 1¼" O.D. metal rings (2); ⅛" Dia. × 26" heavy cord; tung oil (or other penetrating oil finish)

Tools: Jointer, planer, table saw, straightedge, pencil, engineer's square, cordless drill, ³⁄₁₆" and 1" drill bits, 1" brush, lint-free rag

Two Rings Puzzle

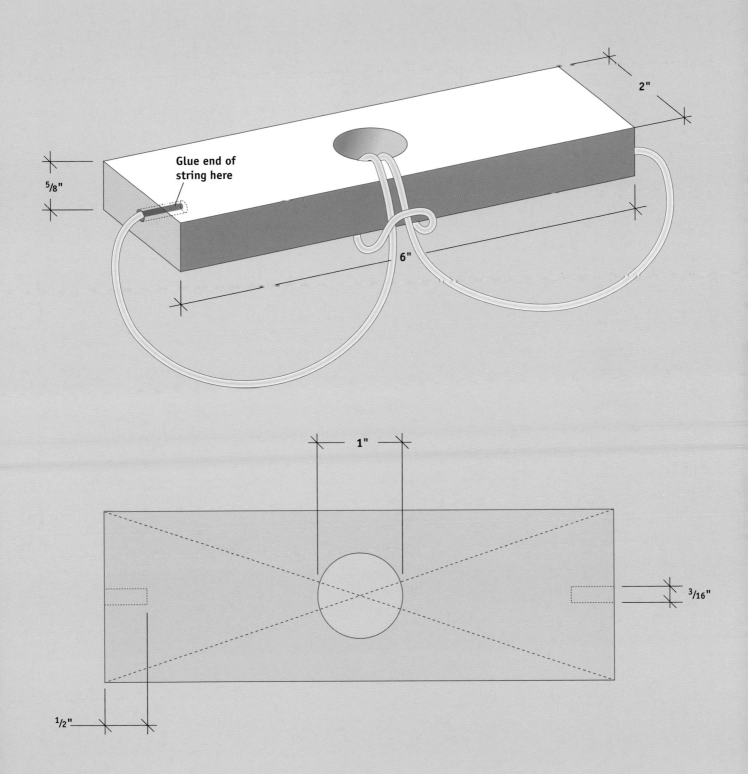

Glue end of string here

5/8"

2"

6"

1"

3/16"

1/2"

How to Make the Two Rings Puzzle

1 To create the puzzle body, joint, plane, and cut down a piece of hardwood to ⅝" × 2" × 6", referring to the illustration on page 37. For basic techniques, see pages 22 to 23. (These are not critical measurements. If you're feeling lazy, use a 6"-long chunk of 1 × 4 instead).

2 Find the centerpoint of the body by drawing a line from one diagonal corner to the other, so that an "X" is formed. Do the same on both ends to find the centerpoints. Drill a 1" hole through the centerpoint on the face of the body. To prevent splintering, clamp the body to a backer board. At the centerpoint of each end, drill a ³⁄₁₆" hole about ½" deep.

3 Use sandpaper to smooth out any rough spots and to smooth the puzzle body. If a finish is desired, apply a modified tung oil, teak oil, or Danish oil using a brush. Or, wipe on with a lint-free rag, following the finish manufacturer's instructions.

4 Fill one of the end holes half-full with yellow glue, then insert an end of the ⅛"-dia., 26"-long cord into the hole. Allow glue to dry for about thirty minutes.

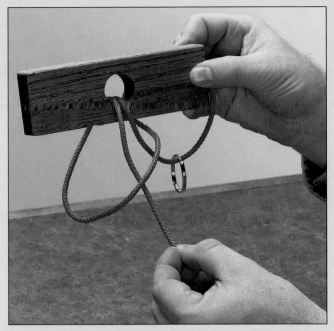

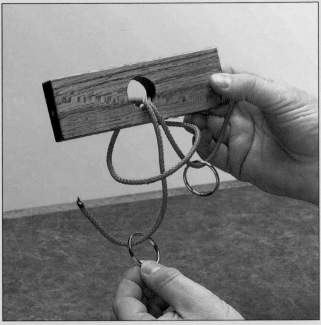

5 Slide a ring onto the cord. Weave the free end of the cord through the front of the center hole and then back through the loop created. The cord is now back at the front of the puzzle. Leaving a little slack in the cord, weave the free end through the back of the center hole to the front of the puzzle, and then back through the second loop created.

6 Slide the second ring onto the cord, then glue the free end of the cord into the hole on the other end of the puzzle. Allow the glue to dry for a day before manipulating the puzzle.

Variation: Puzzle Body Design

The body for the Two Rings Puzzle can be crafted from various materials, in almost any shape or design you can dream up: from an unfinished wood block to a custom shape cut on a scroll saw, even to a spare wooden dowel. Use your imagination to create a personalized puzzle that is all your own.

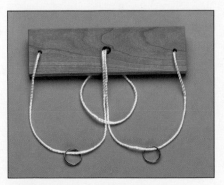

Finished puzzle, simple design: flat board body, ends of cord tied in knot at each end of puzzle.

Finished puzzle: looks like an airplane propeller blade.

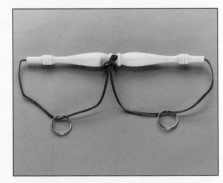

Finished puzzle: a spindle from an old chair gets a new lease on life.

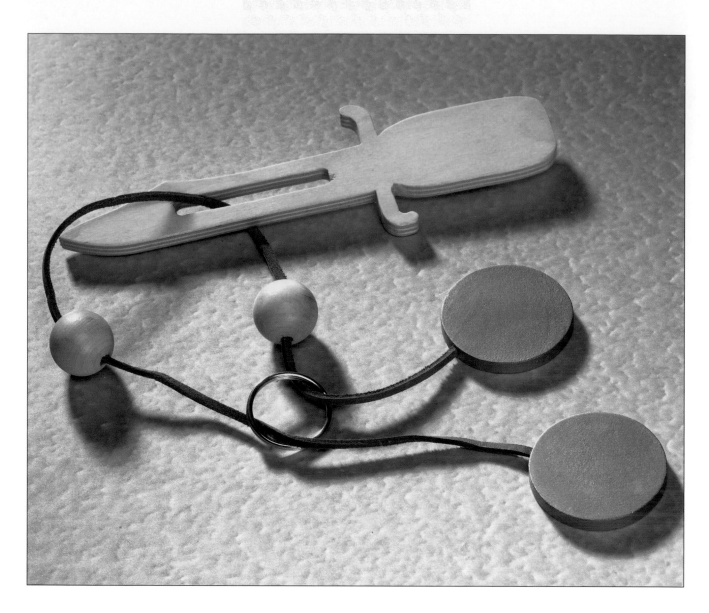

Dagger Puzzle

The Dagger Puzzle is moderately easy to solve and very easy to make. The goal is simply to free the metal ring without cutting the cord. The body of this puzzle can be just about any shape, provided the characteristics of the blade remain: a narrow portion that is slightly thinner than the inside diameter of the ring, a slot in that narrow portion large enough for the discs to pass through, and a stop at the top of the narrow portion that prevents the ring from being removed from the puzzle body.

The Dagger Puzzle is a great beginner's puzzle project because it does not require precise measuring, tight-fitting pieces, or detailed design. Materials are inexpensive and easy to find, and the puzzles can be built rather quickly. However, solving the dagger puzzle may take a little more time. If you find yourself stumped, you can find the solution on page 116.

TOOLS & MATERIALS

Materials: $1/4$" hardwood and $1/2$" Baltic birch, 1" wooden balls, $1^1/4$" inside diameter metal ring, $1/8$"-diameter × 18" cord, quick-release (blue) masking tape, spray clear polyurethane, wood glue

Tools: Cabinetmaker's rule, engineer's square, pencil, scroll saw or small bandsaw, jig saw with fine-tooth blade (18 TPI), cordless drill, drill press, $1/8$" brad-point bit, $3/8$" brad-point bit, $5/8$" Forstner bit, 2" hole saw, 4" handscrew, 3" C-clamp

Dagger Puzzle

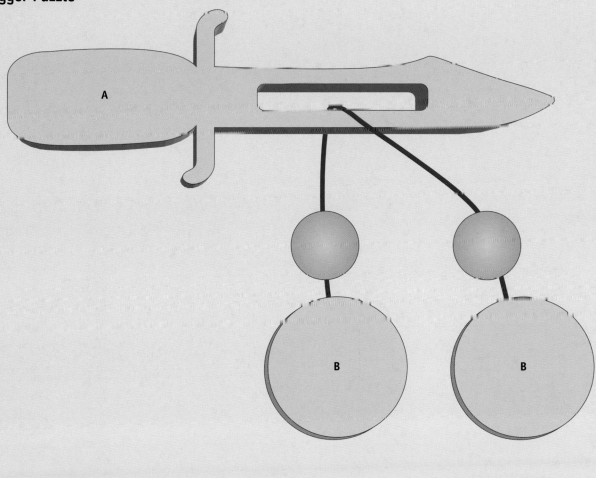

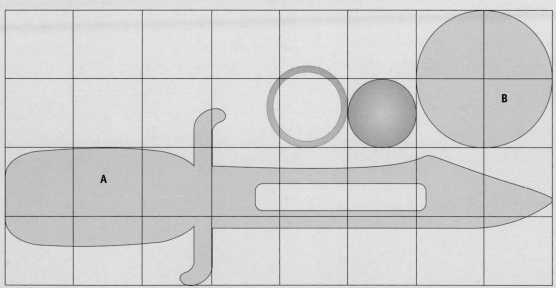

1 sq. = 1 in.

CUTTING LIST:

Key	Part	Size	Material	Number
A	Dagger	$1/2" \times 2^1/2" \times 8"$	Baltic Birch	1
B	Discs	$1/4" \times 2"$-D.	Hardwood	2

How to Make a Dagger Puzzle

Hand guard

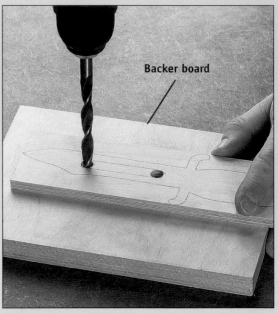

Backer board

1 Lay out the dagger shape on ½" Baltic birch plywood, referring to the illustration on page 41. The blade of the dagger must be slightly thinner than the inside diameter of the metal ring. However, the dagger's hand guard must be larger than the outside diameter of the ring, so the ring stops at the hand guard.

2 Mark the rough location of the slot on the dagger blade, then mark centers for two holes at the ends of the slot, about 3" apart. Drill the holes with a ⅜" brad-point bit, using a backer board to prevent tearout.

3 Cut the dagger body from the plywood, using a scroll saw or small bandsaw. To cut the slot, use a jigsaw with a fine-toothed blade, at least 18 teeth per inch (TPI), to connect the outside edges of the holes. Tip: You can also use a spiral blade on a scroll saw, which makes a very smooth cut.

4 To drill holes through the 1" wooden balls, create the drilling jig found on page 27—clamp a 1½" scrap to the drill press table, then use a ⅞" Forstner bit to drill a ½"-deep hole. Wrap the bottom of each ball with two layers of easy-release (blue) masking tape to reduce splintering, clamp the ball in place, then drill through, using a ¼" bit. Thread the cord through the holes—the balls should move freely along the cord.

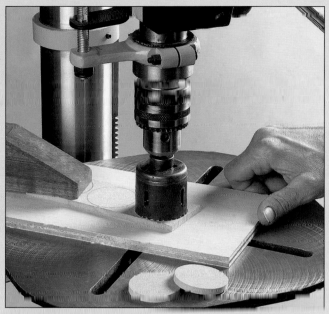

5 To cut the discs, clamp ¼"-thick hardwood and a scrap backer board to the drill press table. Drill through the workpiece using a 2" hole saw with the mandrel (pilot bit) removed. Sand the edges of the discs smooth, then drill ⅛" holes ¼" to ⅜" deep into one edge of each disc for the cord.

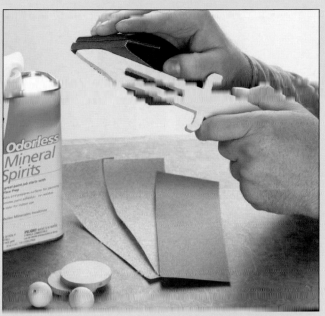

6 Sand all wood parts and round-over sharp edges, starting with 100-grit paper and working up to 150-grit. Also sand the edges of the holes of the wooden balls, as needed. Wipe down all parts with mineral spirits and allow to dry.

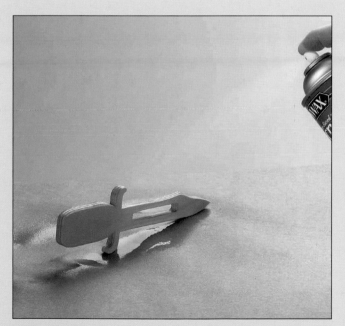

7 Spray the wood parts with polyurethane varnish in your choice of satin or semigloss. Let the finish dry and spray again, applying three light coats. If the polyurethane dries for more than 24 hours before recoating, lightly sand the pieces so the next coat will adhere properly. If you use fast-dry polyurethane (four to six hours), you can apply all three coats in one day.

8 To assemble the puzzle, slip the ring onto the blade of the dagger. Cut 18" of ⅛" cord and glue one end into the hole drilled in one of the discs. Slip a ball on next, then thread the cord through the slot in the dagger blade. On the free end of the cord, slip on the second ball, then glue the cord to the second disc. Once the glue dries, let the ring slide down onto the discs.

Block and Tackle Puzzle

This simple-looking puzzle is created using a block of wood, a pair of wooden balls, and a length of cord. The object of the challenge is to move both balls to the same loop on one side of the block, which is easier said then done. You can find the solution on page 117.

Based on a traditional African puzzle, the Block and Tackle is another in the long line of amazing puzzles designed by noted puzzle-master Stewart Coffin. It is easy to construct from a variety of shapes in a variety of materials. Try using exotic woods like purpleheart or satinwood to add texture to the puzzle. Or, you can substitute metal rings for the wooden balls.

The real trick to making this puzzle is binding the ends of the cord to create one continuous piece. How you accomplish this depends on the size of the cord and the material it's made from. We used thin nylon cord that can be seared and melted together to make a butt joint. If you're using thin cotton string, look for a metal crimp (available at electronic supply stores and some hardware stores) that can be pressed onto the butted end joint with pliers. Whichever method you use, make sure the holes in the block and the wood balls are big enough to let the butted string ends pass through.

Block and Tackle Puzzle

1"
1"
4"
⊄
3/4"
3/4"

Drill the holes at right angles to one another.

TOOLS & MATERIALS

Materials: 1"-thick hardwood, 1½"-dia. wooden balls (2), sandpaper, tung oil, ⅛"-dia. × 24" cotton or nylon cord

Tools: Engineer's square, cabinetmaker's rule, pencil, table saw, drill press, 3/16" and 3/8" drill bits, 1" brush, rag

How to Make the Block and Tackle Puzzle

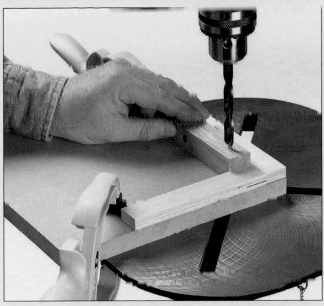

1 Use the table saw to cut a 1" × 1" × 4" block from a piece of hardwood (see pages 22 to 24). Mark a centerline on two adjacent sides of the block. Use a square to measure and mark one hole location ³/₄" in from one end at the centerline, and the other hole location at ³/₄" from the opposite end on the adjacent side—90° off from the first hole (see the illustration on page 44). Drill through the block at each mark, using a ³/₈" bit and a scrap backer board to prevent splintering.

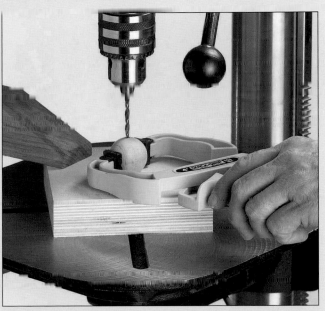

2 Drill holes through the 1¹/₂" wooden balls, using the drilling jig on page 27—clamp a 1¹/₂" scrap to the drill press table, then drill a ¹/₂"-deep hole using a ⁷/₈" Forstner bit. Wrap the bottom of each ball with two layers of easy-release (blue) masking tape to reduce splintering, then clamp the ball in place and drill through, using a ³/₁₆" bit. Test the cord through the holes—the balls should move freely along the cord.

3 Coat all wood parts with tung oil, using a brush or a rag. Wear nitrile gloves to keep the oil off your hands. Wipe off excess oil after a couple of minutes and recoat the pieces. TIP: Drive a pair of 16d nails up through a piece of scrap, set the scrap on your work surface with the nailhead side down and slip the wood balls onto the points to hold them while you apply the finish.

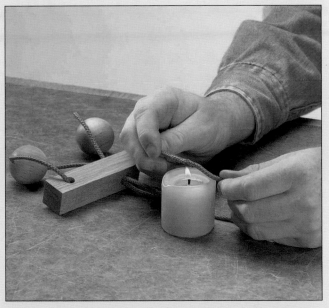

4 Set the block on end and thread the cord through the bottom hole, so there is an equal amount of cord on each side. Slip a wooden ball on each cord, weave both free ends through the front of the top hole, and then wrap each end back around the opposite sides of the block and beneath the cords running into the top hole. If you're using nylon cord, you can join the ends by searing them over a flame until they melt together.

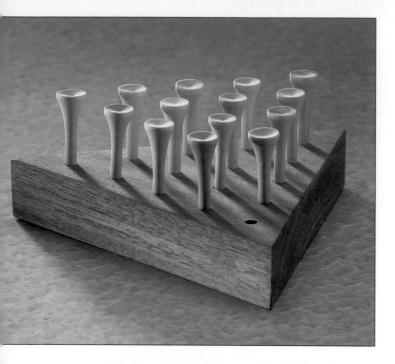

Peg Solitaire

Peg Solitaire is perhaps the most familiar puzzle in this book. This traditional game can be found in a variety of forms across the U.S. and around the world. The object is to remove pegs from the base by jumping and removing other pegs until only one remains. You may jump one peg at a time and only to a free hole. You may not move a peg if you are not jumping another peg. For an extra challenge, see if you can jump pegs so the last one ends up in the center hole.

This Peg Solitaire puzzle is made from a 5" triangular base cut from teak. It contains fifteen equally spaced peg holes located by bisecting the triangle and the triangles formed thereafter. With the addition of wooden golf tees for pegs, the result is a rather attractive puzzle. Because of the familiarity of this puzzle and the numerous ways it can be solved, we have not provided a solution. But keep at it—you'll get it eventually.

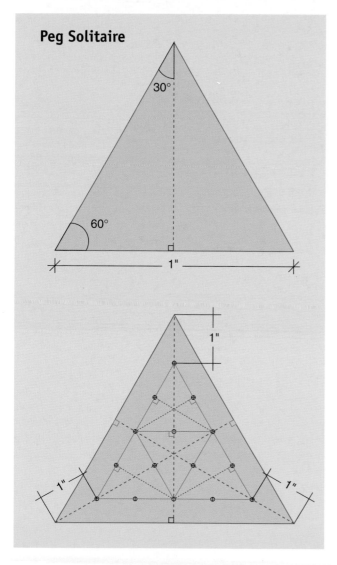

Peg Solitaire

TOOLS & MATERIALS
Materials: 1" × 6" teak, wooden golf tees (15), 150-grit sandpaper, teak oil
Tools: table saw or miter saw, combination square, drill press, $^3/_{16}$" drill bit, 1" brush or lint-free rag

How to Make the Peg Solitaire Puzzle

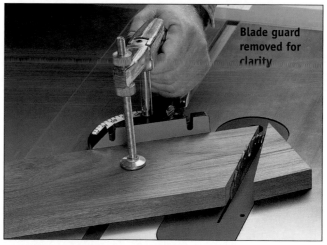

Blade guard removed for clarity

1 Rip your hardwood stock (teak is used here) to 5" in width. Adjust the miter gauge to 60°, then cut at the top of the board to create the first leg of the triangle. Or, set your power miter saw to 30° and make the cut.

Blade guard removed for clarity

2 Move the miter gauge to the opposite miter slot on the table saw and flip the board over. Leaving the miter gauge set at 60°, cut the base from the board. Each side of the base should measure 5", forming an equilateral triangle.

3 To lay out the peg holes, use a ruler to bisect the triangle on all three sides, as shown in the bottom illustration on page 46. At each point of the base, measure in 1" increments along the bisect lines and mark, then connect those points with a pencil. Mark the six locations where the lines cross, connect those points to create smaller triangles, and then bisect those triangles to locate the remainder of the equidistant peg hole locations (15 total).

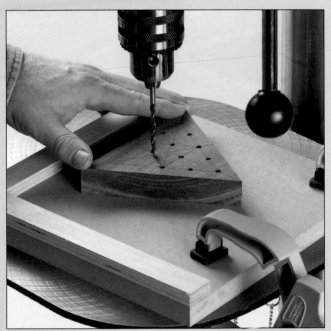

4 Mount a $^3/_{16}$" drill bit in a drill press and set the depth-stop on the drill press to $^1/_2$". Check the depth with a scrap and insert a golf tee to check that the hole depth and diameter are correct. Make adjustments as needed, then drill the holes into the base.

5 Lightly sand the triangle base to remove pencil lines, then apply several coats of teak oil, following the manufacturer's instructions. Keep the flow light so the holes don't gum up with excessive finish. Allow to dry, then insert the golf tees. Note: You may need to cut the golf tees down to size.

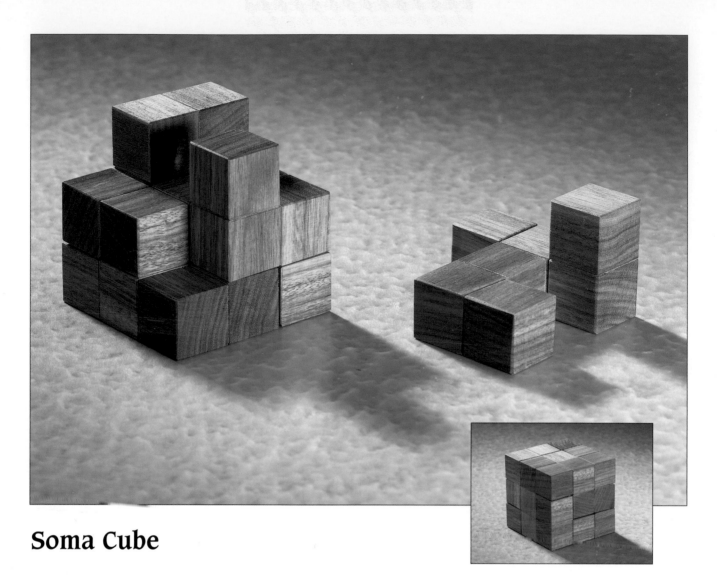

Soma Cube

During a lecture on mathematics in the mid-1930s, Danish poet and inventor Piet Hein began to imagine the variety of ways in which three and four cubes can be assembled, other than in straight lines. He discovered there were seven distinct shapes comprised of a total of 27 cubes. Mr. Hein then realized that those shapes would fit together to create a larger, perfect cube. And thus was born the Soma Cube.

Named for the soma drug in Aldous Huxley's *Brave New World*, it has been proven that there are exactly 240 uniquely different ways to configure the seven pieces into a cube. And much like the dreamlike effects produced by the drug in the book, attempting to unlock the many possible solutions can be highly addictive. In fact, there is even a newsletter for the most rabid of Soma fans. While we have provided one of the possible solutions on page 118, finding the rest is up to you.

Constructing the Soma Cube pieces is not a difficult task, but creating perfect wooden cubes does take some practice. Make sure your table saw blade is true and your crosscut jig is accurate. Use a scrap piece to set the jig's length stop, then check cube dimensions using calipers. When gluing up pieces, use small amounts of glue to ensure the finished pieces remain proportional to one another. For this project, we have also included instructions for creating an attractive cube storage case.

TOOLS & MATERIALS

Materials: $1/4"$ × 4" and 1" × 4" hardwood, wood glue, sandpaper (various grits), tung oil

Tools: Jointer, planer, table saw, engineer's square, cabinetmaker's rule, marking knife, dial calipers, crosscut jig, clamps, single-edged razor blade, brush or lint-free rag

Soma Cube

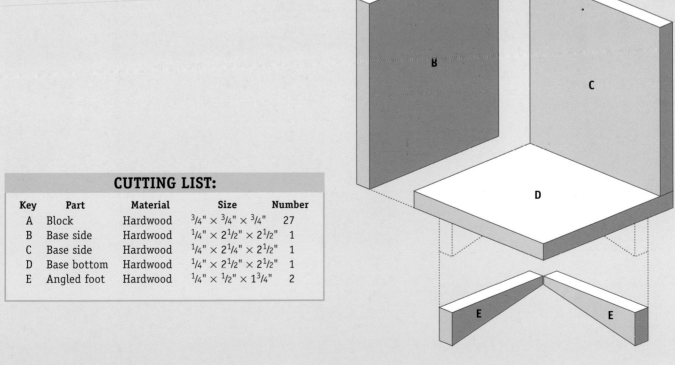

3/4" (dimensions shown on piece 6)
3/4"
3/4"

1
2
3
4
5
6
7

A
B
C
D
E
E

CUTTING LIST:

Key	Part	Material	Size	Number
A	Block	Hardwood	$3/4" \times 3/4" \times 3/4"$	27
B	Base side	Hardwood	$1/4" \times 2^{1}/2" \times 2^{1}/2"$	1
C	Base side	Hardwood	$1/4" \times 2^{1}/4" \times 2^{1}/2"$	1
D	Base bottom	Hardwood	$1/4" \times 2^{1}/2" \times 2^{1}/2"$	1
E	Angled foot	Hardwood	$1/4" \times 1/2" \times 1^{3}/4"$	2

How to Make the Soma Cube

1 Mill hardwood stock to $3/4$" × $3/4$" and clamp it to the back rail of your crosscut sled so a piece exactly $3/4$" long will be trimmed off when the workpiece is fed into the blade.

2 Clamp a stop block to the back rail so it is flush against the workpiece and then remove the workpiece clamp. You're now set up to make repetitive, uniform cuts for creating the 27 $3/4$" × $3/4$" × $3/4$" cubes.

3 Double-check the dimensions of the first cube with calipers and adjust the setup if needed. Cut all 27 cubes, plus a few extra in case you get tearout on any of the cubes.

4 Arrange each series of cubes according to the illustrations on page 49. Assembly of the entire puzzle is easier if pieces are laid out before gluing. Try to orient the cubes so the grain is running in the same direction on each shaped piece.

5 Glue up each of the seven shapes. Place just a dab of glue on the cube face, spread with a stick, and slide the glued faces together. You can remove glue squeezeout while it's still wet using a single-blade razor blade. Use the gluing jigs on pages 30 to 31 to ensure square joints. Apply light clamping pressure.

6 Once the glue has dried, assemble the pieces into the cube to test the fit (see Solutions, page 118). Lightly sand the game pieces. If the pieces do not fit tightly, make new ones as needed.

TIP BOX:

TIP: Puzzle making almost always involves small parts. If you glue two wood pieces and they somehow slip or slide out of position while the glue dries, put them in the microwave for 20 to 40 seconds (try low setting first) and they can be twisted apart and reglued. This trick will work up to an hour after pieces are glued together. Always wear gloves when you grab pieces as they will be hot. Let them cool before working with them again.

7 Finish the pieces as desired. You may wish to stain the pieces contrasting colors (if you have used a single wood species), or simply finish them with penetrating oil. Because these game pieces will be handled extensively, you'll want a good finish to protect against oily hands.

Half-hour Puzzle

With its 27 $\frac{3}{4}$" cubes knitted into a larger cube shape, The Half-hour Puzzle may look like a Soma Cube (pages 48 to 53) on the surface. But where the Soma can be assembled with at least 240 configurations of its seven pieces, the Half-hour Puzzle has only one solution. Another creation of puzzle-master Stewart Coffin, this game cube gets its name from the average amount of time an experienced puzzle enthusiast takes to solve it (see page 118).

The process for building the Half-hour Puzzle is practically identical to the way you make the Soma Cube, so if you're planning to take on the project, read that section, too. To add some dimension to this project, we've included instructions for a simple box to hold the puzzle (see page 57).

Visual interest can be added to the Half-hour Puzzle by using woods such as rosewood contrasted with hard maple. Purple heart also makes a fine contrast, especially with yellow heart.

TOOLS & MATERIALS

Materials: $\frac{1}{4}$" and 1" hardwood, wood glue, 150-grit sandpaper, penetrating oil

Tools: Jointer, planer, engineer's square, cabinetmaker's rule, marking knife, table saw, calipers, crosscut jig, single-edge razor blade, 1" brush, lint-free rag

Half-hour Puzzle

1

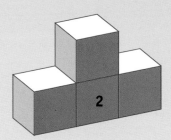

2

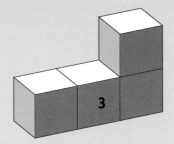

3

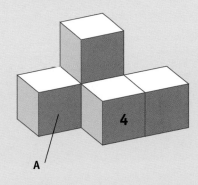

A

4

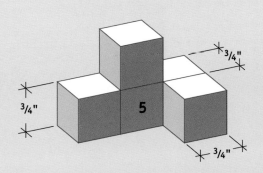

3/4"

3/4"

5

3/4"

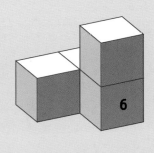

6

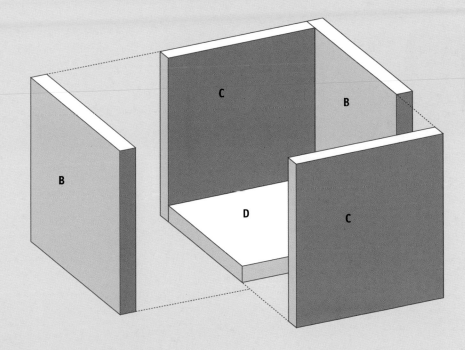

B

C

B

D

C

CUTTING LIST:

Key	Part	Size	Material	Number
A	Basic block	$3/4" \times 3/4" \times 3/4"$	Hardwood	27
B	Box side	$1/4" \times 2 3/4" \times 2 1/2"$	Hardwood	2
C	Box side	$1/4" \times 2 5/16" \times 2 1/2"$	Hardwood	2
D	Box base	$1/4" \times 2 5/16" \times 2 5/16"$	Hardwood	1

How to Make the Half-hour Puzzle

1 Mill hardwood workpieces to ³/₄" × ³/₄" and set up your crosscut jig to cut off ³/₄" cubes (see page 50). Cut 27 cubes (plus a couple of extras) and sand them lightly to smooth out saw marks.

2 Assemble the cubes into the puzzle shapes, following the diagram on page 55. Arranging the cubes before gluing makes the process easier.

3 Spread a small amount of glue on the mating faces of the cubes and then slide the glued faces against each other. Assemble the cubes into the six dissimilar shapes, using the gluing jig shown on pages 30 and 31 to help alignment and provide a surface for light clamping.

4 After the glue has dried for 24 hours, assemble the puzzle pieces to test the fit (see the solution on page 118). Lightly sand pieces as needed to create a perfect 2¹/₄" cube, but do not remove so much stock that the pieces are no longer proportional. If the pieces do not fit tightly, remake them as needed. Finally, apply a finish (we used penetrating oil).

How to Make a Box for the Half-hour Puzzle

1 A simple storage box will help you keep track of the pieces in the Half-hour Puzzle. Cut four sides and a base to size from ¼"-thick hardwood on the table saw. Refer to the cutting list on page 55 to find the dimensions for the box pieces.

2 Use wood glue to construct the box. Apply glue lightly around the edges and use clamps as needed to hold the box together as it dries. Allow the glue to cure overnight.

3 Test-fit the finished pieces of the Half-hour Puzzle into the box. The puzzle should sit flush with the top edge of the box. Carefully sand the box as needed to soften sharp edges and smooth the overall piece.

4 Apply penetrating oil to finish the box, following the manufacturer's instructions. Make sure to wipe excess oil from the interior of the box to ensure the cube will fit.

Four-piece Interlocking Cube

Another of the many amazing puzzles designed by Stewart Coffin, this unique interlocking puzzle must be solved serially—that is, in the correct order (solution is on page 118). This is also a 27-cube puzzle, with glued-up pieces fitting together snugly. Because of the complexity of the four shapes created by the ¾" cubes, the glue-up is more difficult for this puzzle than for the Half-hour or Soma puzzles. The gluing jig on pages 30 and 31 will be especially useful for the project.

To create a slight variation in appearance from the Soma and Half-hour puzzles, we sanded the edges of each individual cube to break the surface and create a faceted appearance similar to dice. To accomplish this, we hand sanded each edge for two strokes (see photo, page 60). If you prefer to use power tools, clamp a belt sander to your work surface with the sanding belt facing up. Cut a ½"-wide × 1"-long slot in a piece of ¼"-thick scrap. Position the scrap so it just touches the spinning sanding belt, then press each cube edge through the slot (centered) to remove a uniform amount of wood from each edge.

TOOLS & MATERIALS

Materials: 1"-thick hardwood, wood glue, 150-grit sandpaper, tung oil

Tools: Jointer, planer, engineer's square, cabinetmaker's rule, marking knife, table saw, dial caliper, crosscut jig, single-edge razor blade, brush, lint-free rag

Four-piece Interlocking Cube

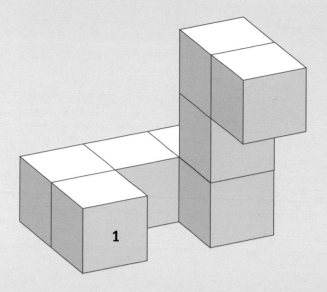

1

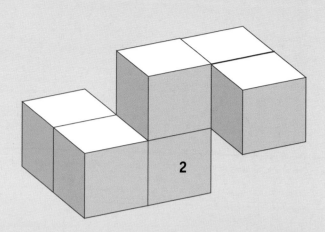

2

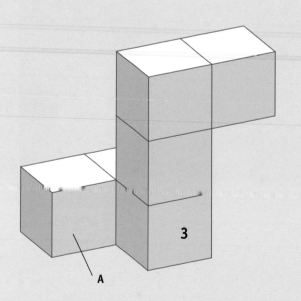

3

A

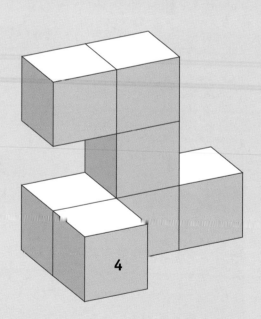

4

CUTTING LIST:				
Key	**Part**	**Material**	**Size**	**Number**
A	Block	Hardwood	$^3/_4" \times {}^3/_4" \times {}^3/_4"$	27

Six-piece Burr Puzzle

The Six-piece Burr Puzzle captures very nicely the fun of puzzle making. It is made up of six notched sticks that fit together to form a knot shape when the puzzle is solved (see page 119). Although the six uniquely shaped pieces look relatively complicated, you can cut them with just four settings on a table saw with a dado-blade set. For this project, you'll definitely want to make and use the notching jig featured on pages 18 to 19.

Yet another offfering designed by Stewart Coffin, the Six-piece Burr Puzzle will challenge your ability to think spatially in a new way—during the construction process, as well as when you try to solve

it. We made our version of birch with a medium walnut oil finish. If you find that you enjoy making and solving this puzzle, we think you'll also like the Boxed Burr Puzzle on pages 84 to 89.

TOOLS & MATERIALS

Materials: $3/4" \times 3/4" \times 2^{1}/4"$ hardwood (6), 150-grit sandpaper, tung oil

Tools: Cabinetmaker's rule, dial caliper, marking knife, adjustable square, planer, table saw with dado-head or blade set (stackable blades are preferable), miter gauge, small hand and spring clamps, sanding block, brush

Six-piece Burr Puzzle

Top face

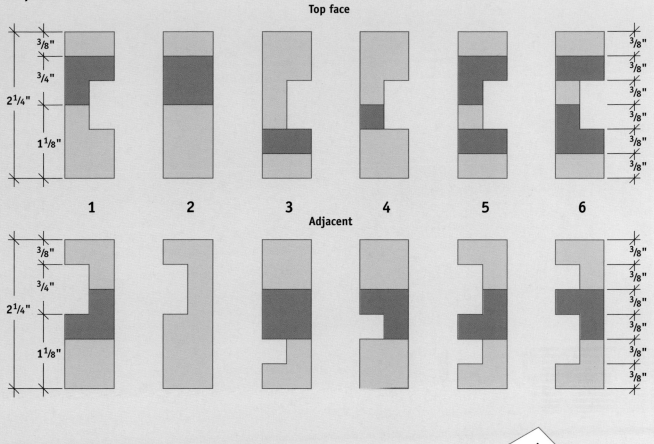

1   2   3   4   5   6

Adjacent

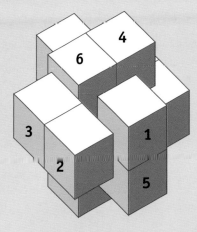

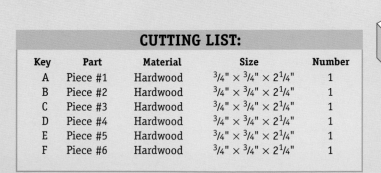

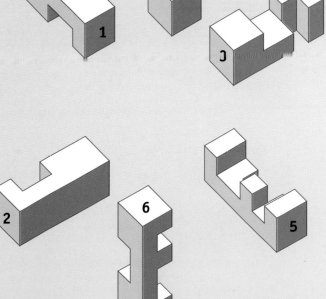

CUTTING LIST:				
Key	Part	Material	Size	Number
A	Piece #1	Hardwood	$3/4" \times 3/4" \times 2^1/4"$	1
B	Piece #2	Hardwood	$3/4" \times 3/4" \times 2^1/4"$	1
C	Piece #3	Hardwood	$3/4" \times 3/4" \times 2^1/4"$	1
D	Piece #4	Hardwood	$3/4" \times 3/4" \times 2^1/4"$	1
E	Piece #5	Hardwood	$3/4" \times 3/4" \times 2^1/4"$	1
F	Piece #6	Hardwood	$3/4" \times 3/4" \times 2^1/4"$	1

How to Make the Six-piece Burr Puzzle

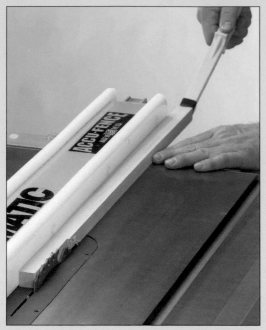

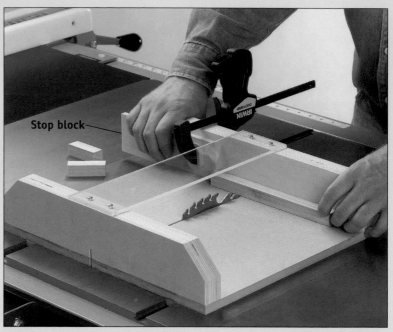

1 Mill hardwood into ³/₄" × ³/₄" sticks. For this puzzle you'll need about two lineal feet of stock.

2 Clamp a scrapwood stop block to the back rail of the crosscut jig (pages 15 to 17), positioned 2¹/₄" from the table saw blade. Cut six 2¹/₄"-long puzzle pieces.

3 Using a pencil, lightly label the ends and faces of the six puzzle pieces and number them 1 through 6 for reference. You'll also find it helpful to map out the pieces on a sheet of paper (or copy the artwork from page 67) and place them in their appropriate spot to keep track of the notch cuts.

4 Outfit the table saw with a dado-blade set that's set to cut a ³/₄"-wide notch. Adjust the blade height to ³/₈", then make a test cut on a piece of scrap, using the notching jig (pages 18 to 19).

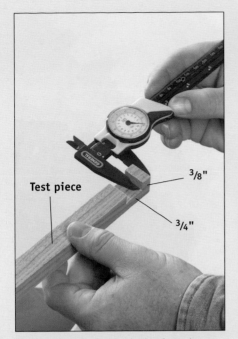

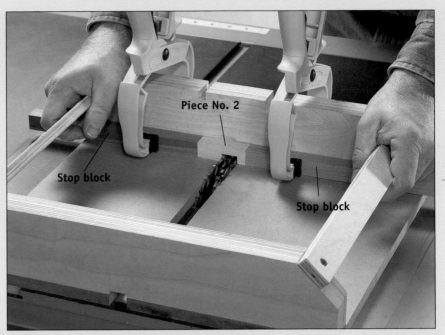

5 Clamp a stop block that's at least 4" wide to the back rail of the notching jig, ³/₈" from the dado blade. Make a test cut—the test piece should have a ³/₄" notch that starts ³/₈" from the end. Make adjustments to stop as needed.

6 Four of the six pieces (1, 2, 5, 6) are cut with a full-width (³/₄") notch starting ³/₈" from one end. Place each of these four parts against the orginal stop block from Step 5, and then clamp a second block firmly against the free end of the workpiece to sandwich it it in place. Cut the ³/₈"-deep notch in each of the four pieces. For a smooth, clean cut, make two or three passes, deepening the notch cut with each pass. Piece No. 2 is finished.

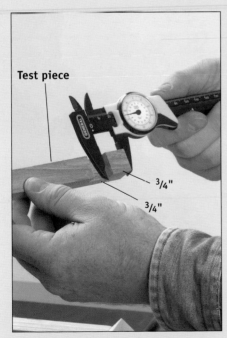

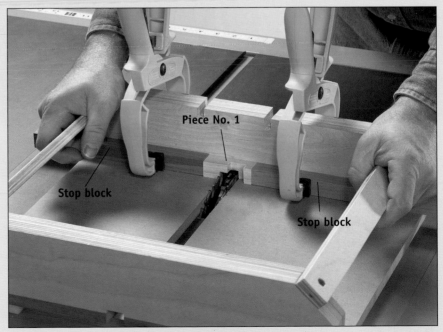

7 Reset the stop blocks to cut a notch that begins ³/₄" from the end of the workpiece. Test your set-up on a piece of scrap.

8 All five of the remaining pieces receive a ³/₄"-wide notch ³/₄" from one end. Sandwich the pieces between stop blocks, one at a time, and cut the notches carefully, using the illustrations on page 67 as guides. Piece No. 1 is finished.

How to Make the 24-piece Chuck Puzzle

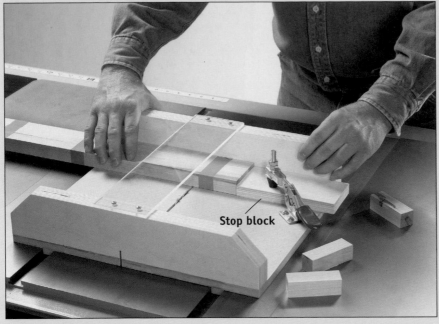

1 For efficient cutting of the blanks to make the 24 puzzle pieces, mill stock to create three 1" × 1" × 36" sticks. Gang them together (use easy-release masking tape to bind them for cutting) and cut the pieces to length using a stop block clamped to the crosscut jig (pages 15 to 17). You'll need 18 3"-long pieces and six 6"-long pieces.

2 Outfit the table saw with a dado-blade set. Since most sets have a maximum cutting width of ³/₄" or ⁷/₈", you'll need even the narrowest (1") notches in multiple passes. Set up the dado blades to make ³/₄"-wide × ¹/₂"-deep cuts.

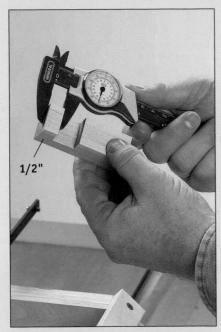

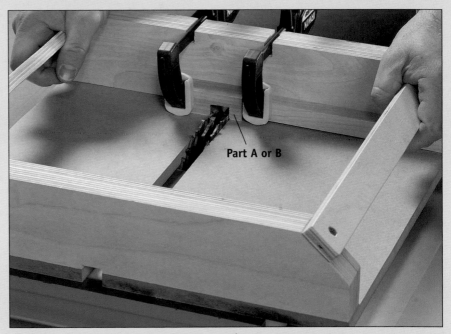

3 Clamp a stop block to the back rail of a notching jig (see pages 18 to 19). Check with caliper to make sure the setup is accurate.

4 All 24 pieces have notches that start ¹/₂" from each end. Position the blank for each piece against the stop and clamp the workpiece to the back rail of the jig, keeping clear of the blade set. Make a pass over the blade set at both ends of each workpiece, on the same face.

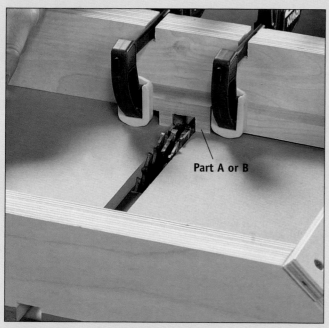

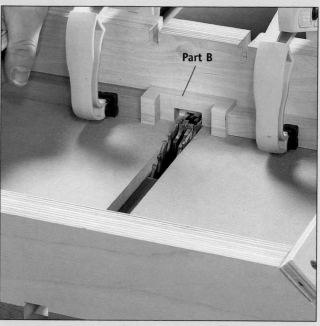

5 Finish cutting all of the 16 small bridge pieces (Part A, page 77) by shifting the stop block and hogging out the waste wood between the notches cut near each end. Make the same cuts on the two pieces that will become the keys (Part B, page 77).

6 Finish notching the two keys by positioning them between stop blocks and cutting a 1"-wide notch, centered, on an adjoining face to the one that has been notched already.

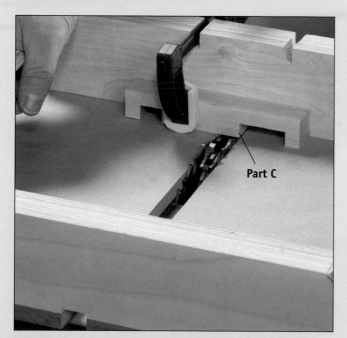

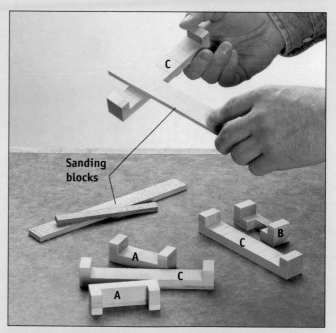

7 Make the six large bridge pieces (Part C, page 77) by passing each piece over the dado blade to hog out the waste material between the notches near each end. This can be done without a stop block to speed up your work.

8 Lightly sand all the pieces, and test-fit following the solution on page 121. Pieces should fit together snugly. Take care not to round the edges when sanding pieces. Apply a penetrating oil to finish, following the manufacturer's instructions.

How to Make the Notched Packing Puzzle

1 Mill your wood stock to ³⁄₄" × ³⁄₄" to make the blanks for the 18 2¹⁄₄"-long puzzle pieces (a pair of 36"-long sticks is plenty of stock). Set up a stop on a crosscut jig (pages 15 to 17) and cut the blanks to uniform length.

2 Outfit the table saw with a dado-blade set adjusted to make a ³⁄₄"-wide × ³⁄₈"-deep notch cut.

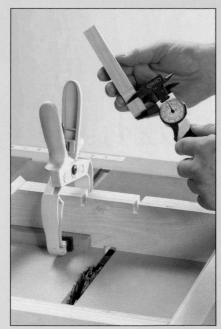

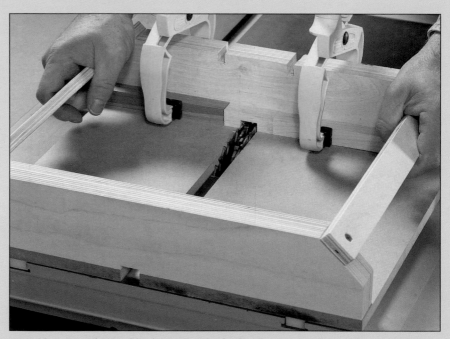

3 Set up a notching jig (pages 18 to 19) with a stop block that's ³⁄₄" from the dado-blade set. Cut a notch on a piece of scrap and measure to make sure it is ³⁄₈" deep, ³⁄₄" wide, and centered on the puzzle piece.

4 Add a second stop block so the blanks for the puzzle pieces fit snugly between stop blocks. Notch all 18 pieces, making at least two passes at full cutting depth for a smooth bottom on the notch cut.

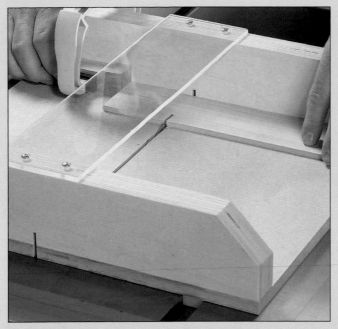

5 Cut the ends, sides, and bottom for the box to size from 1/4"-thick hardwood, using the table saw and a cross-cut jig. Refer to the cutting list on page 81 for dimensions of box pieces.

6 Use wood glue to construct the box, following the technical illustration on page 81. Apply glue lightly to the edges and use clamps as needed to hold the box together while the glue dries.

7 Test-fit the puzzle pieces in the box, following the solution on page 122. The pieces should sit flush with the top edge of the box. Carefully sand the box and pieces as needed to soften sharp edges, smooth the overall piece, and ensure a snug fit. TIP: If you assemble the pieces outside of the box, it's much easier to fit the upside-down box over the rectangular solid than to lower the asssembled pieces into the box.

8 Apply penetrating oil to finish the puzzle pieces and box, following the manufacturer's instructions. Apply only one or two coats to avoid adding dimension to the parts.

Box for Solid Cube Pentominoes

OVERALL SIZE:
$3^5/8" \times 4^3/8" \times 2^1/2"$

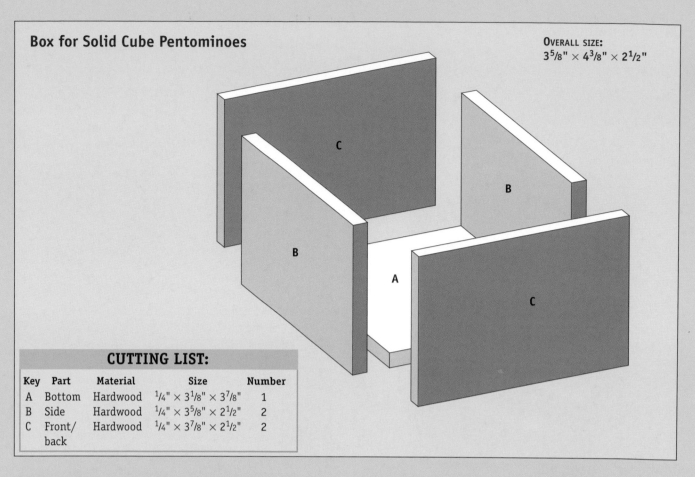

CUTTING LIST:

Key	Part	Material	Size	Number
A	Bottom	Hardwood	$^1/4" \times 3^1/8" \times 3^7/8"$	1
B	Side	Hardwood	$^1/4" \times 3^5/8" \times 2^1/2"$	2
C	Front/back	Hardwood	$^1/4" \times 3^7/8" \times 2^1/2"$	2

How to Make a Box for the Solid Pentominoes Cube Puzzle

Cut the sides, front, back, and bottom pieces to size according to the dimensions shown above. Apply wood glue to the joints between the pieces and assemble, checking for square and clamping together into a box shape. Make sure all joints are flush and square. Allow glue to dry overnight.

Lightly sand the base, then test-fit the pieces, following the solution on page 123. Pieces should fit snugly but be easy to remove. Carefully sand the inside edge of the sides and ends to make adjustments, then apply a penetrating oil, following the manufacturer's instructions.

Base for 2D Pentominoes

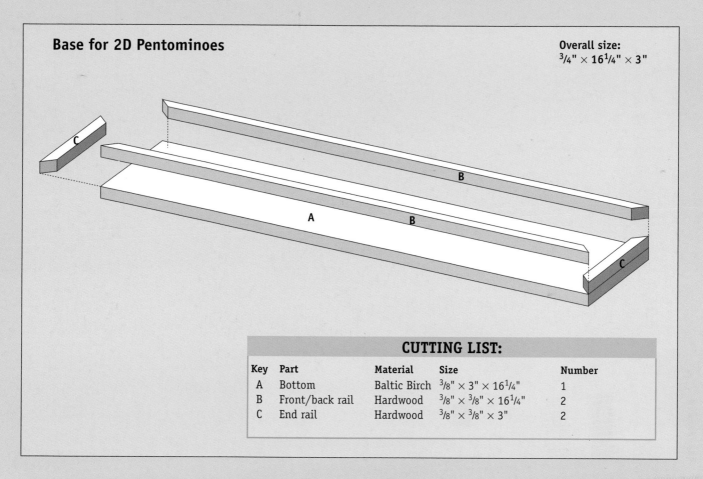

CUTTING LIST:

Key	Part	Material	Size	Number
A	Bottom	Baltic Birch	$3/8" \times 3" \times 16^{1}/4"$	1
B	Front/back rail	Hardwood	$3/8" \times 3/8" \times 16^{1}/4"$	2
C	End rail	Hardwood	$3/8" \times 3/8" \times 3"$	2

How to Make a Base for the 2D Pentominoes Puzzle

Mill hardwood stock to $3/8" \times 3/8"$ thickness and miter-cut ends at 45° to the lengths shown above to make rails. Cut base from Baltic birch or hardwood and glue rails to base.

Lightly sand the base, then test-fit the Pentominoes pieces, following the solution on page 123. Pieces should fit snugly but be easy to remove. Carefully sand the inside edge of the sides and ends to make adjustments, then apply a penetrating oil, following the manufacturer's instructions.

Twin Homes Puzzle

The Twin Homes Puzzle is unlike any other in this book. The goal is pretty simple—fit the puzzle pieces together so they fit inside the gable-topped house frame. But there is more to the puzzle than that. If you flip the house frame over, you'll find another frame that looks like the first but is actually sized a bit differently. The solution that works for the first side will not work for the opposite side.

Construction of the two-sided house is accomplished by gluing all the parts for each side to the divider panel (at slight offsets from one another) and then cutting the final house shape from the glued-up parts on the table saw.

Another offering from noted designer Stewart Coffin, the Twin Homes Puzzle proves that even as houses today look more and more alike, there are often subtle differences that are easy to overlook. Solutions on page 123.

TOOLS & MATERIALS

Materials: $3/4" \times 3/4" \times 24"$ hardwood, $1/4" \times 1" \times 60"$ hardwood, $1/4" \times 8" \times 9"$ hardwood or Baltic birch plywood, wood glue, sandpaper, teak or Danish oil

Tools: Cabinetmaker's rule, dial caliper, pencil or marking knife, adjustable square, planer, table saw, miter saw or table saw miter jig (to cut miters), brush

Twin Homes Puzzle (Side A)

Overall size:
$3/4" \times 5 1/4" \times 6"$

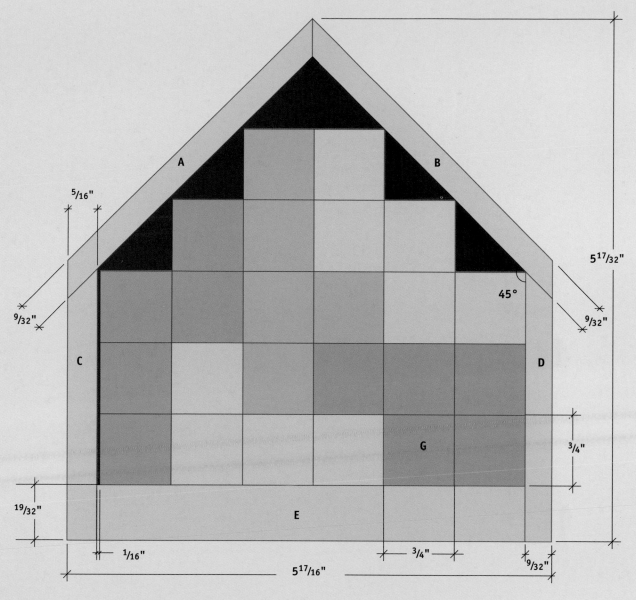

$5/16"$

$5^{17}/32"$

$9/32"$

A

B

$45°$

$9/32"$

C

D

$3/4"$

G

$19/32"$

E

$1/16"$

$3/4"$

$9/32"$

$5^{17}/16"$

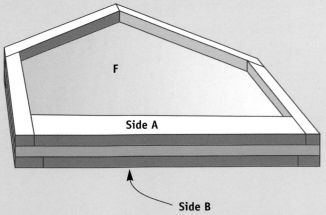

F

Side A

Side B

CUTTING LIST (SIDE A):

Key	Part	Material	Size	Number
A	Rafter, left	Hardwood	$1/4" \times 9/32" \times 4"$	1
B	Rafter, right	Hardwood	$1/4" \times 9/32" \times 4"$	1
C	Wall, left	Hardwood	$1/4" \times 5/16" \times 3"$	1
D	Wall, right	Hardwood	$1/4" \times 9/32" \times 3"$	1
E	Floor	Hardwood	$1/4" \times 19/32" \times 4^9/16"$	1
F	Divider	Hardwood or plywood	$1/4" \times 5^5/32" \times 6"$	1
G	Puzzle pieces	Hardwood	$3/8" \times 3/4" \times 3/4"$	24

Twin Homes Puzzle (Side B)

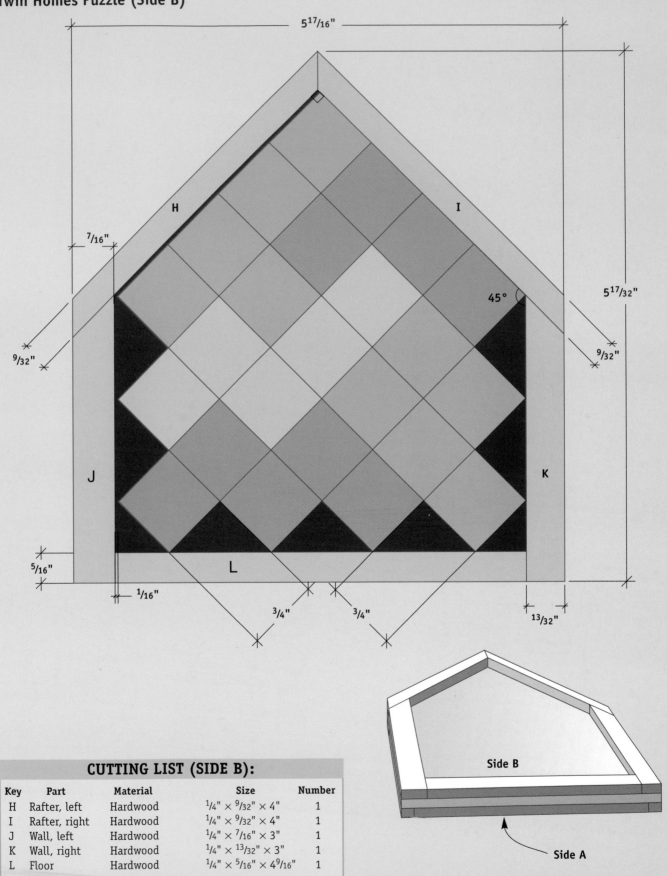

$5^{17}/_{16}$"

$5^{17}/_{32}$"

H

I

45°

J

K

L

$7/_{16}$"

$9/_{32}$"

$9/_{32}$"

$5/_{16}$"

$1/_{16}$"

$3/_4$"

$3/_4$"

$13/_{32}$"

Side B

Side A

CUTTING LIST (SIDE B):

Key	Part	Material	Size	Number
H	Rafter, left	Hardwood	$1/_4$" × $9/_{32}$" × 4"	1
I	Rafter, right	Hardwood	$1/_4$" × $9/_{32}$" × 4"	1
J	Wall, left	Hardwood	$1/_4$" × $7/_{16}$" × 3"	1
K	Wall, right	Hardwood	$1/_4$" × $13/_{32}$" × 3"	1
L	Floor	Hardwood	$1/_4$" × $5/_{16}$" × $4^9/_{16}$"	1

How to Make the Twin Homes Puzzle

Blade guard removed for clarity

1 Following the techniques on pages 22 to 24, mill hardwood stock for the puzzle pieces to ³/₄" × ³/₄".

2 Clamp a stop block ³/₈" from the blade and cut 24 ³/₈"-thick puzzle pieces, using a crosscut jig (see pages 15 to 17). For safety, shut off the saw and remove the cut square after each cut.

3 Lightly sand the edges of the cubes with 150-grit sandpaper. Tape a section of sandpaper flat to the work surface, then simply draw each edge of a cube across the sandpaper twice. The result gives each cube a cleaner, polished appearance.

4 Arrange the squares into the figures shown in the illustration on page 97. Wipe on a dab of glue and rub the pieces together, then set in the square corner gluing jig for at least an hour under light clamping pressure. Make sure the glued pieces lie flat. To prevent possible sticking to the workbench, use a nonstick work surface, coat the benchtop with paste wax, or slip wax paper under the glued-up pieces.

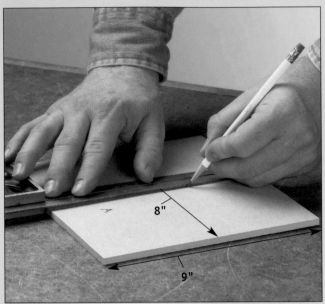

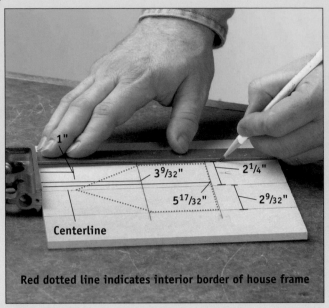

Red dotted line indicates interior border of house frame

5 Cut a ¼"-thick piece of hardwood or Baltic birch ply-wood to 8" × 9" to use for the divider. Label one face "A" and the other "B". Begin making layout lines by scribing a centerline that bisects the 9" sides on both faces of the workpiece. Lay out the interior dimensions for the first puzzle on Side A: Measure down from the top along the centerline and mark at 1", 3⁹⁄₃₂", and 5¹⁷⁄₃₂".

6 Measure out from the 5¹⁷⁄₃₂" and mark one side at 2⁹⁄₃₂" and the other at 2¼". Do the same at the 2⁹⁄₃₂" mark along the centerline. Use the square to connect the dots and form the lower rectangular half of the puzzle house.

7 Make a 45° miter cut at one end of eight ¼"-thick × 1"-wide hardwood sticks so each stick is at least 6" in length. These will be used to make the walls and rafters for both Side A and Side B. Glue the mitered ends of two pairs together to create a 90° corner of the roof pitch, and allow the glue-up to dry. Set one roof assembly and two of the side pieces aside for Side B.

8 Glue the roof assembly on one side of the divider panel so the inside angle of the roof peak hits the 1" mark on the centerline, and the inside edges of the rafters intersect the second layout line. Glue two wall frame pieces along the sides of the layout rectangle with the mitered ends butted against the rafters. Fit the puzzle parts into the house to test the fit.

9 With the puzzle parts still in place, measure between the walls, and cut a $\frac{1}{4}$" × 1"-wide stick to fit. Glue it to the the divider panel, so there is a $\frac{1}{32}$" gap between the puzzle pieces and the bottom edge. Remove the puzzle pieces and lay a flat, heavy object (such as an encyclopedia) onto the pieces to clamp them and hold them in place while the glue dries.

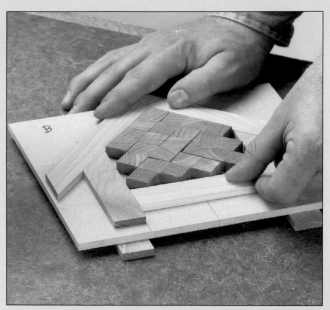

10 Make layout lines for Side B the same way as for Side A (Steps 5 and 6), but with slightly different measurements. Measuring down from the top along the centerline, mark points at 1", $3\frac{1}{8}$", and $5\frac{25}{32}$". Measure out $2\frac{5}{32}$" and $2\frac{1}{8}$" on each side of the $5\frac{25}{32}$" mark. Do the same at the $3\frac{1}{8}$" mark. Repeat the rest of the Side A steps to complete the framing for side B.

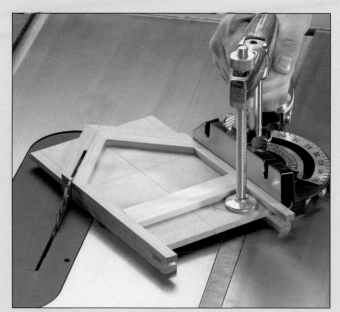

11 Cut the puzzle down to size using your table saw's miter gauge and a hold-down clamp (or you could use a power miter saw). The illustrations on pages 97 and 98 provide the finished dimensions you'll need to cut to.

12 Lightly sand the Twin Home frame on all sides and also sand the puzzle pieces. Test-fit the pieces to make sure they fit snugly, but can easily be removed. Finish the puzzle and pieces using a penetrating oil, following the manufacturer's instructions.

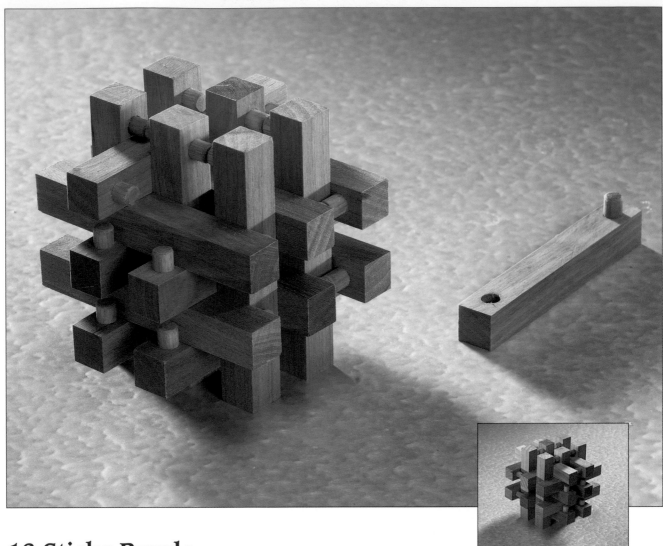

18 Sticks Puzzle

The 18 Sticks Puzzle is comprised of 18 ½" × ½" wood sticks (17 are identical) and 35 dowel pins. The dowels serve as linchpins to hold the polyhedron shape created by the puzzle pieces together. The last dowel to be inserted has a pin on one end only and is the key to the puzzle solution.

We made the puzzle seen here out of maple stock with ¼"-dia. maple dowels. You can use just about any hardwood you choose. One attractive combination would be walnut pieces with contrasting maple or oak dowels. You can also vary the size if you wish. It is important that you maintain the same proportions between the sizes of the parts and the spacing. If you make the thickness of the puzzle pieces (½" as shown) one unit, then the length should be seven units (3½" as shown) and the spacing between the inside edges of the dowel pin holes should be five units (2½" as shown).

As with many other puzzles, the trick to solving the 18 Sticks Puzzle is the sequence in which you join the pieces. The solution can be found on page 124.

TOOLS & MATERIALS

Materials: ½" × ½" × 72" hardwood, ¼" × 24" hardwood dowel, wood glue, tung oil

Tools: Jointer, planer, engineer's square, cabinetmaker's rule, marking knife, table saw, dial caliper, crosscut jig, drill press, ¼" drill bit, miter saw, miter box, clamps, brush, lint-free rag

18 Sticks Puzzle

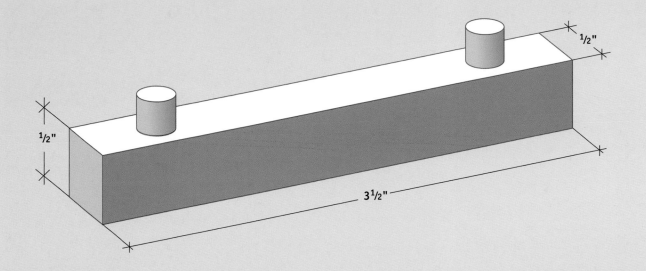

CUTTING LIST:				
Key	Part	Size	Material	Number
A	Stick	$1/2" \times 1/2" \times 3^1/2"$	Cherry or walnut	18
B	Dowel peg	$1/4"$ dia. $\times 1/2"$	Birch or maple	35

How to Make the 18 Sticks Puzzle

1 Mill your hardwood stock to ¹/₂" × ¹/₂" sticks and cut 18 sticks to 3¹/₂" long using a crosscut jig (see pages 15 to 17).

2 Make a drilling jig (see pages 26 to 27) and position one of the sticks into the corner where the jig rails meet. Mark a drilling point that's centered lengthwise on the stick, ³/₈" from the end. With a ¹/₄" brad-point or Forstner bit mounted in your drill press, align the stick so the drilling point is directly under the bit spur, and clamp the jig to the drill press table.

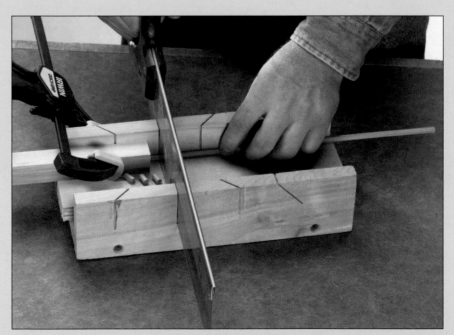

3 Set the drill press depth stop to drill a hole that's ¹/₄" deep. Flip the piece end-for-end and drill another hole. The centers of the holes should be 2¹/₂" apart. Drill holes in both ends of 17 of the pieces, leaving one piece with only one hole (this will be the key piece).

4 Cut 35 ¹/₂"-long pieces from a length of ¹/₄"-dia. hardwood doweling. For safe, clean cuts, use a hand miter box and fine-tooth backsaw to make the cuts. A stop block ensures uniform length of parts. Lightly sand the ends of the dowels to clean up the cuts and create a slight bevel all the way around (this will help you insert the dowel and prevent splintering).

5 Apply glue to one end of each dowel pin and insert the pins into the dowel holes in the puzzle pieces. Press the dowels firmly so they are fully seated in the holes.

6 After the glue has dried, assemble the pieces to create the polyhedron shape (see solution on page 124). If the pieces do not fit together properly, the inside faces of the dowels can be sanded until the fit is snug.

7 Finish the project with penetrating oil.

Tower of Hanoi

The goal of this ages-old three-post puzzle is to move all of the discs or chips from one end post to the other. Start with the game pieces stacked in decreasing size from top to bottom on one end post. Moving only one piece at a time, you must transfer the stack. This would be very easy except for one stipulation: You may never place a larger piece on top of a smaller piece.

Sold in toy stores as far back as the 1880s, the Tower of Hanoi puzzle can contain just about any number of pieces, which determines the level of difficulty (the more pieces, the harder it is to solve). The version shown here has eight square chips made from ¼"-thick maple. More traditional puzzles are made with disc-shaped pieces that can be cut with a set of hole saws. In case you're stuck, the basic strategy for moving pieces is shown in three photos on page 124.

basic strategy for moving pieces is shown in three photos on page 124.

TOOLS & MATERIALS

Materials: ³/₄" × 5" × 13" hardwood board, ³/₈"-dia. × 24" hardwood dowel, ¼" × 4¼" × 28" hardwood board, glue, sandpaper, paint, stain, tung oil

Tools: Jointer, planer, table saw, drill press, miter box, miter saw, brush, rag, square, rule, pencil

Tower of Hanoi

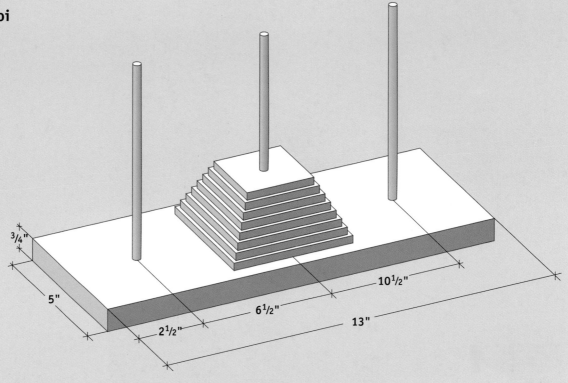

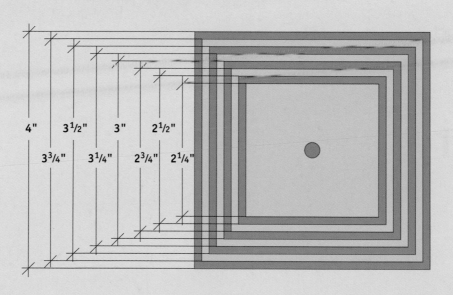

CUTTING LIST:

Key	Part	Size	Material	Number
A	Base board	$^3/_4 \times$ "5" $\times$ 13"	Hardwood	1
B	Post	$^3/_8$"-dia. $\times$ 7"	Hardwood	3
C	Chip	$^1/_4$" $\times$ 4"	Hardwood	1
D	Chip	$^1/_4$" $\times$ 3$^3/_4$" $\times$ 3$^3/_4$"	Hardwood	1
E	Chip	$^1/_4$" $\times$ 3$^1/_2$" $\times$ 3$^1/_2$"	Hardwood	1
F	Chip	$^1/_4$" $\times$ 3$^1/_4$" $\times$ 3$^1/_4$"	Hardwood	1
G	Chip	$^1/_4$" $\times$ 3" $\times$ 3"	Hardwood	1
H	Chip	$^1/_4$" $\times$ 2$^3/_4$" 2$^3/_4$"	Hardwood	1
I	Chip	$^1/_4$" $\times$ 2$^1/_2$" 2$^1/_2$"	Hardwood	1
J	Chip	$^1/_4$" $\times$ 2$^1/_4$" 2$^1/_4$"	Hardwood	1

How to Make the Tower of Hanoi Puzzle

1 Using a miter box and backsaw, cut three 7" lengths of $1/4$"-dia. doweling to make the posts for the game board. Round one end of each piece with sandpaper.

Blade guard removed for clarity

2 Cut the game board for the puzzle to size ($3/4$" × 5" × 13"). For a finished appearance, round-over the top edges of the game board with a router and $1/8$" roundover bit. Alternately, ease them with a sander.

3 Mark the baseboard with a line down the center lengthwise. Mark points at $2^1/2$", $6^1/2$" and $10^1/2$" from one end. Drill $13/32$" holes that are $1/2$" deep at each point to make guide holes for the dowel posts.

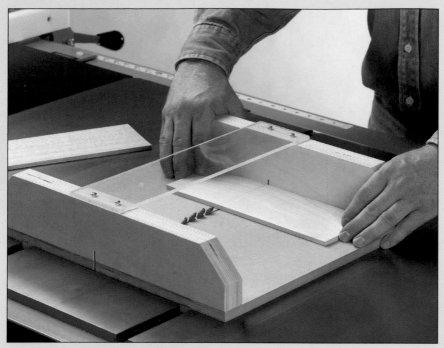

4 Cut the playing pieces (the chips or discs) to their final dimensions (see page 107). A table saw with a crosscut jig (see pages 15 to 17) makes this job safer. Be sure to use a hold-down to secure the workpiece when cutting smaller parts.

5 Mark a centerpoint on each playing piece and mount a 5/16" drill bit in your drill press. Drill through each playing piece. Use a square corner drilling jig (see page 26) or a clamp to hold the disks steady as you drill.

6 Glue the dowel posts into their holes, using a small amount of wood glue. Wipe up any excess or squeezed-out glue with a damp cloth immediately.

7 Finish or paint the playing pieces as desired. Make certain finish does not collect in the center holes as this will affect the fit.

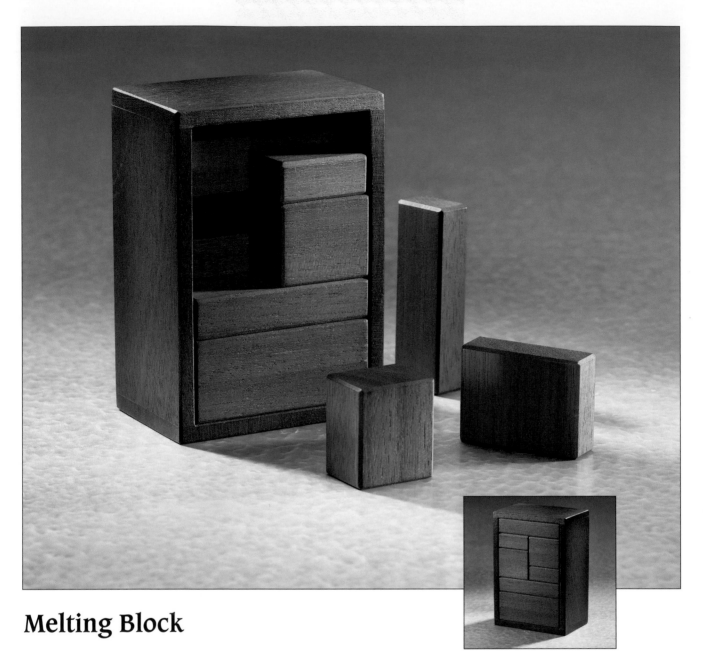

Melting Block

Nine blocks of wood fit snugly into a rectangular solid inside this box to complete the Melting Block. When built with a rich hardwood, like the Honduran mahogany seen here, the puzzle has an exotic, captivating appearance. Solving it isn't especially difficult, so it's a great choice for younger kids (but they should be at least three years old—like most of the puzzles in this book, the Melting Block has small parts that pose choking hazards).

Building this puzzle can be a little tricky because you'll need to cut the wood stock into small, unique shapes with virtually no margin for error. But all of the parts are designed so they can be cut from stock that's thicknessed to $^{19}/_{32}$" with a planer. Figuring out how to make the pieces as efficiently as possible is a bit of a puzzle in itself. The solution to the Melting Block is on page 123.

TOOLS & MATERIALS

Materials: $^{1}/_{2}$" × 4" × 24" hardwood for blocks, $^{1}/_{4}$" × 3" × 18" hardwood for box, wood glue, tung oil

Tools: Jointer, planer, table saw, bandsaw (or scroll saw or hand saw), dial caliper, crosscut jig, brush, rag, square, rule, pencil

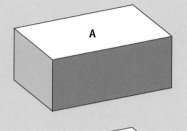

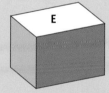

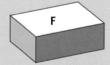

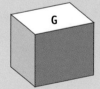

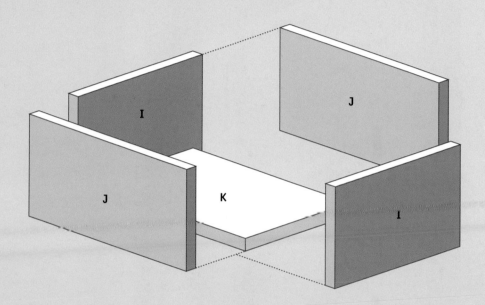

CUTTING LIST:

Key	Part	Size	Material	Number
A	Block	$1^3/16" \times 1^{13}/16" \times 2^3/4"$	Hardwood	1
B	Block	$^{19}/32" \times 1^{13}/16" \times 2^3/4"$	Hardwood	1
C	Block	$^{29}/32" \times 1^3/16" \times 2^3/4"$	Hardwood	1
D	Block	$^{19}/32" \times ^{29}/32" \times 2^3/4"$	Hardwood	1
E	Block	$1^3/16" \times 1^3/8" \times 1^{13}/16$	Hardwood	1
F	Block	$^{19}/32" \times 1^3/8" \times 1^{13}/16"$	Hardwood	1
G	Block	$^{29}/32" \times 1^3/16" \times 1^3/8"$	Hardwood	1
H	Block	$^{19}/32" \times ^{29}/32" \times 1^3/8"$	Hardwood	2
I	Box end	$^1/4" \times 3^5/16" \times 2"$	Hardwood	2
J	Box side	$^1/4" \times 4^1/8" \times 2"$	Hardwood	2
K	Box bottom	$^1/4" \times 4^1/8" \times 2^{13}/16"$	Hardwood	1

How to Make the Melting Block Puzzle

1 Prepare wood stock for the puzzle pieces. All the pieces can be cut or glued up from slices of a 4" × 24" piece of hardwood that's been thickness-planed to $^{19}/_{32}$" thick. Use a dial caliper for precise thickness measurements. We used Honduran mahogany for the puzzle shown here. Plane stock to $^1/_4$" thick for making the box.

2 Face-glue some of the $^{19}/_{32}$"-thick stock into $^{13}/_{16}$"-thick blocks. If you examine the cutting list on page 111, you'll see that every puzzle piece has one dimension that's either $^{19}/_{32}$" (one layer) or $^{13}/_{16}$" (two layers)—note that this dimension is not always the thickness.

3 Cut the blocks into the finished puzzle sizes shown on page 111. Crosscuts on some of the larger pieces may be done with a table saw and crosscut jig (see pages 15 to 17). But more delicate cuts on smaller workpieces require a bandsaw, scroll saw, or handsaw. Cut all nine puzzle pieces to size, sand them, and see if you can assemble them into a rectangular solid (see solution on page 123).

4 Following the illustration and cutting list on page 111, cut the pieces for the puzzle box, and glue them together. Use small hand clamps as needed to hold pieces in place and allow the box to dry overnight.

5 Test-fit the pieces in the box. The inside dimension of the box should be no more than $1/32$" larger in width and length then the blocks when they are in the rectangular solid form. Blocks should fit snugly but still be easy to remove.

6 For added detail, carefully sand or round off the edges of the blocks. Finish the nine blocks and box with tung oil, following the manufacturer's instructions.

Wood Puzzle Solutions

So, you couldn't solve it, eh? If you must, here are the solutions to the puzzles...well, most of them, anyway. We've left the solution to Peg Solitaire up to you—it's really more of a game than a puzzle and there are many routes to the goal. As for the other puzzles, the solutions are found on the following pages. If you can, though, try not to give in to temptation and peek. The fun is in the frustration, so it's best to keep these pages far from sight when playing with the puzzles. The point of these brainteasers is to put your problem-solving skills to the test. If the solutions are readily available, where's the challenge? Allow your mind to work out the solutions, and you'll be rewarded with satisfaction, accomplishment, and bragging rights over all those people who can't solve your wood logic puzzles.

Pages 36 to 39: Two Rings Puzzle

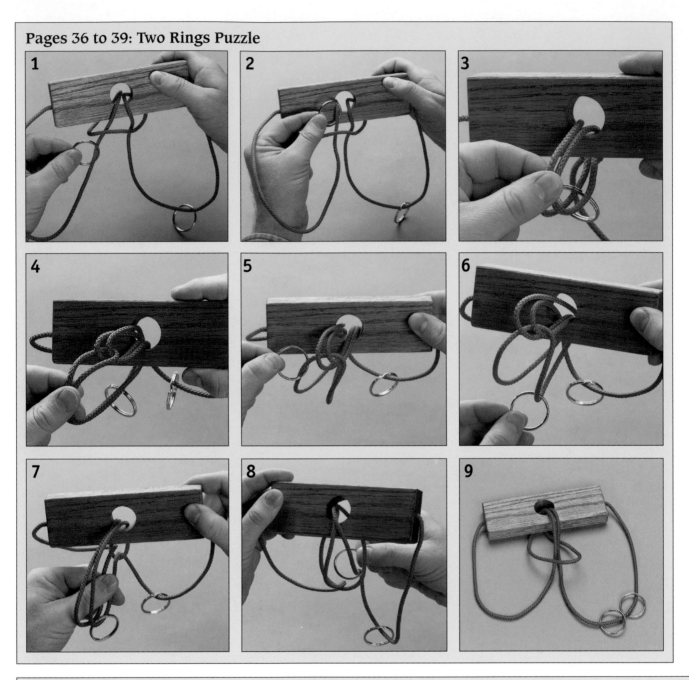

Pages 40 to 41: Dagger Puzzle

Pages 44 to 45: Block and Tackle Puzzle

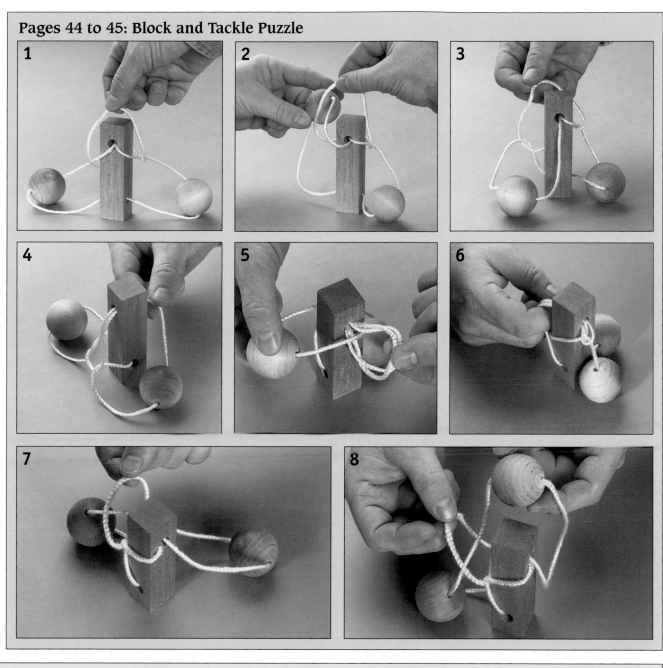

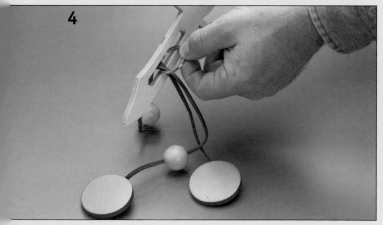

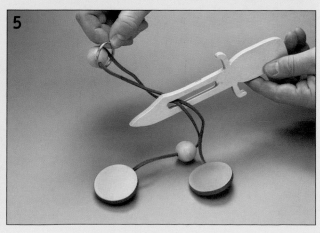

Pages 48 to 53: Soma Cube (1 of 240 solutions)

1

2

3

4

Pages 54 to 57: Half-hour Puzzle

1

2

3

4

Pages 58 to 61: Four-piece Interlocking Cube

1

2

3

4

Pages 62 to 65: Wooden Knot

1

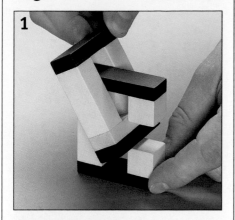

2

3

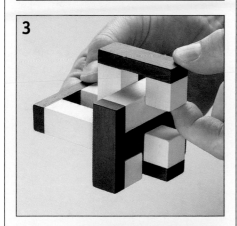

4

Pages 66 to 71: Six-piece Burr Puzzle

1

2

3

4

5

6

Pages 72 to 75: Altekruse Puzzle

1

2

3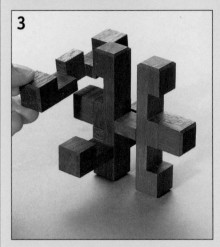

4

5

6

7

8

Pages 76 to 79: 24-piece Chuck Puzzle

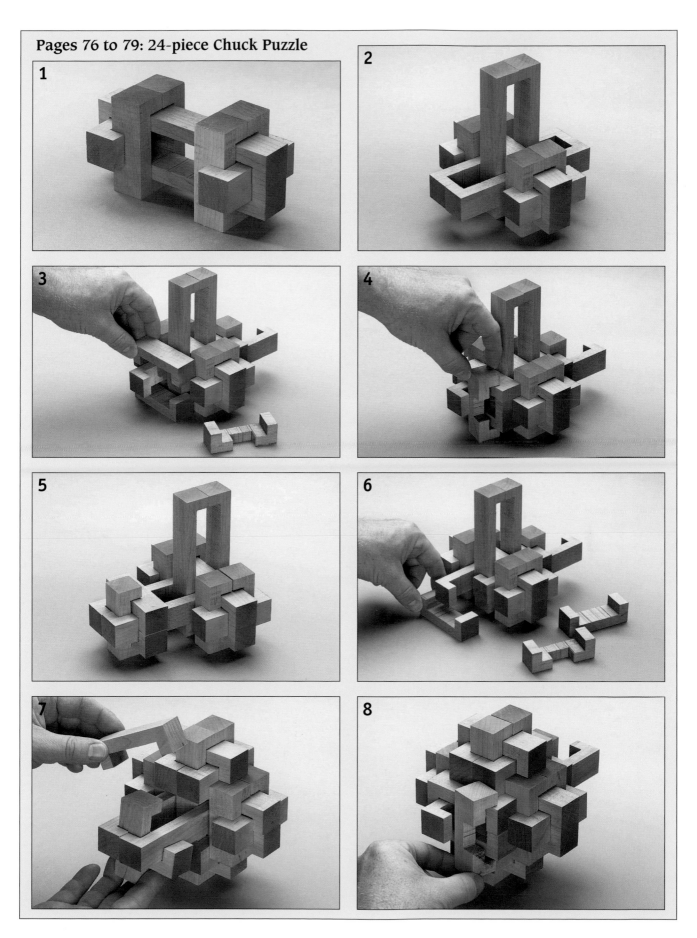

Pages 80 to 83: Notched Packing Puzzle (1 of 12 solutions)

1

2

3

4

5

Pages 84 to 89: Boxed Burr Puzzle

1

2

3

4

5

6

Pages 90 to 95: Pentominoes Solid Cube Puzzle
(1 of 2940 solutions)

1

2

3

4

5

Page 95: Pentominoes 2D Base

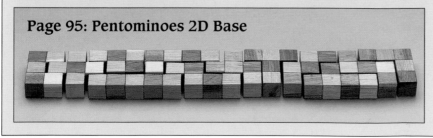

Pages 96 to 101: Twin Homes Puzzle

Side A

Side B

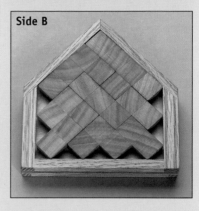

Pages 110 to 113: Melting Block

1

2

Pages 102 to 105: 18 Sticks

1

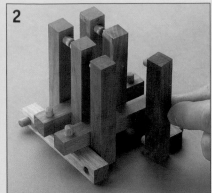

2

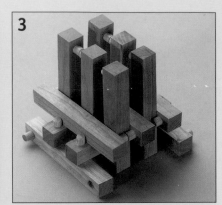

3

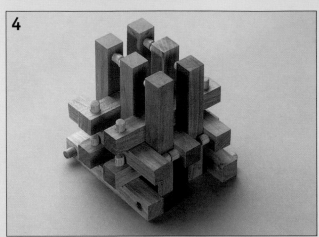

4

5

6

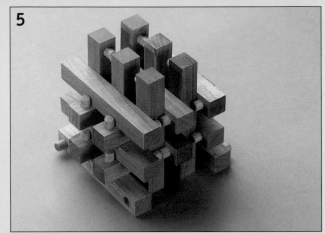

7

Pages 106 to 109: Tower of Hanoi

1

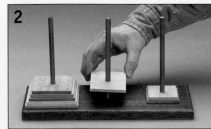

2

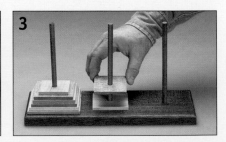

3